The Precious Blood of Jesus

STUDY GUIDE

The Precious Blood of Jesus

STUDY GUIDE

By Dr. Kevin L. Zadai

Please note that Warrior Notes publishing style capitalizes certain pronouns in Scripture that refer to the Father, Son, and Holy Spirit, which may differ from some publishers' styles. Take note that the name "satan" and related names are not capitalized. We choose not to acknowledge him, even to the point of violating accepted grammatical rules. All emphasis within Scripture quotations is the author's own.

Cover design: Virtually Possible Designs

For more information about our school, go to www.warriornotesschool.com. Reach us on the internet: www.Kevinzadai.com

ISBN 13 TP: 978-1-6631-0016-0

Dedication

I dedicate this book to the Lord Jesus Christ. When I died during surgery and met with Jesus on the other side, He insisted that I return to life on the earth and that I help people with their destinies. Because of Jesus' love and concern for people, the Lord has actually chosen to send a person back from death to help everyone who will receive that help so that his or her destiny and purpose is secure in Him. I want You, Lord, to know that when You come to take me to be with You someday, it is my sincere hope that people remember not me, but the revelation of Jesus Christ that You have revealed through me. I want others to know that I am merely being obedient to Your Heavenly calling and mission, which is to reveal Your plan for the fulfillment of the divine destiny for each of God's children.

Acknowledgments

In addition to sharing my story with everyone through the books *Heavenly Visitation: A Guide to the Supernatural, Days of Heaven on Earth: A Guide to the Days Ahead, A Meeting Place with God, Your Hidden Destiny Revealed, Praying from the Heavenly Realms: Supernatural Secrets to a Lifestyle of Answered Prayer, The Agenda of Angels, Supernatural Finances, Receiving From Heaven, You Can Hear God's Voice, The Mystery of the Power Words,* and *The Notes of a Warrior,* the Lord gave me the commission to produce this book, *Holy Fire.* This book addresses some of the revelations concerning the areas that Jesus reviewed and revealed to me through the Word of God and by the Spirit of God during several visitations. I want to thank everyone who has encouraged me, assisted me, and prayed for me during the writing of this work, especially my spiritual parents, Dr. Jesse Duplantis and Dr. Cathy Duplantis. Special thanks to my wonderful wife Kathi for her love and dedication to the Lord and me. Thank you, Sid Roth and staff, for your love of our supernatural Messiah, Jesus. Thank you to a great staff for the wonderful job editing this book. Special thanks, as well, to all my friends who know about *The Notes of a Warrior* and how to operate in this for the next move of God's Spirit!

Contents

Introduction...1

Chapter 1 Blood Shed For The Remission of Sins...3

Chapter 2 The Inheritance and Covenant We Have In God......................15

Chapter 3 There Is Life In The Blood...29

Chapter 4 The Blood Is Powerful Enough To Make You Righteous..............41

Chapter 5 Partakers of God's Inheritance...51

Chapter 6 Holy and Blameless...63

Chapter 7 Grounded and Steadfast...77

Chapter 8 Fellowship with God...89

Chapter 9 Blessed Communion...103

Chapter 10 The Manifestation of Faith..117

Introduction

I am very excited to share on this subject and take you through this study. Since I was a young Christian, I have noticed that the demonic spirits hate the blood of Jesus which is why I have been studying this topic for many years!

Though this study I want you to gain understanding of how God thinks and operates. We can see God's plan for sacrifice and redemption from the very beginning. God instituted blood sacrifices and showed man the process, all in preparation for Christ's blood sacrifice on the cross; and it did not end there, His blood is continually working! Christ's blood has a voice, and it speaks to the Father, it declares that we have been purchased, and that we are His. We are the redeemed of the Lord!

God is calling you to a deeper level of revelation through this study on *The Precious Blood of Jesus*. It is time to implement these truths in your own life, as well as teach them to others in preparation for the next move of our Father God.

CHAPTER ONE

Blood Shed for the Remission of Sin

But Christ came as High Priest of the good things to come, with the greater and more perfect tabernacle not made with hands, that is, not of this creation. Not with the blood of goats and calves, but with His own blood He entered the Most Holy Place once for all, having obtained eternal redemption. For if the blood of bulls and goats and the ashes of a heifer, sprinkling the unclean, sanctifies for the purifying of the flesh, how much more shall the blood of Christ, who through the eternal Spirit offered Himself without spot to God, cleanse your conscience from dead works to serve the living God? And for this reason He is the Mediator of the new covenant, by means of death, for the redemption of the transgressions under the first covenant, that those who are called may receive the promise of the eternal inheritance.

—Hebrews 9:11-15 NKJV

DISCUSSION:

There is a process to how God thinks, and there's a reason why God requires blood. With the inception of sin in the garden, sacrifice was brought in when God gave the skins of animals to Adam and Eve. It was the initial indication that animals had given their lives and blood was shed for the sin that came in through Adam and Eve. The animal skins didn't just appear; it was God's sign that sacrifice was needed. We see how blood addresses the demonic; they flee. We know that blood has a voice from when Cain killed Abel and his blood cried out to God (Genesis 4:10). We see how Moses received from God on the mountain and found that life is in the blood (Leviticus 17:11). In the New Testament, we see how Jesus' blood was shed on the cross and how He became the sacrifice for us (Hebrews 10:1-10).

THE HIGH PRIEST

- Before Jesus, the high priest would go into the Holy of Holies one time per year.
- Within the tabernacle there was an outer court, inner court, and the Holy of Holies was the most holy place.
- Aaron was the first high priest (Numbers 17:5-9).
- When Moses was in the cleft of the rock, God told Moses what God's name is (Exodus 34:5). He was the first person to receive the name of God.
- Moses told Aaron the name when he became high priest, and Aaron passed it on.
- As each new high priest was brought in, they were also given the name of God.

- They were only allowed to speak His name once a year, with blood, in the Holy of Holies.

- It was for the sins of Israel every year.

- Now, Christ is our high priest (Hebrews 4:14).

- It is His blood being presented in the Holy of Holies.

- He is the eternal priest, and He will never be replaced.

What is the significance of the high priest using of blood within the Holy of Holies?

_____

_____

_____

_____

- Jesus became the high priest, and the Bible says He is likened unto Melchizedek because Christ is eternal (Hebrews 7:15).

- Melchizedek didn't have a birth date or a death date. He doesn't have any records. They just know he existed, but he was not born and did not die (Hebrews 7:3).

- He appeared with no beginning and no end.

- He was one of the judges on the earth prior to Moses receiving the law.

- The purpose of a judge was to bring law and order into the different cities to keep them from going into chaos too quickly.

- When the law came, that was the curb for sin.

- We still live by different laws and boundaries today.

- It's because people won't do the right thing on their own.

- People need to have an incentive, or else they fear punishment if they do something wrong.

- We have laws and police officers in place because people won't walk in love and do the right thing on their own.

- Before Moses, there was a mysterious group of individuals who were the ruling class.

- They were eternal beings, just like the elders that you read about in the book of Revelation. It doesn't say that they were human. It doesn't say they were Angels either.

- Scripture talks about the creatures in heaven, and we don't always know what they are.

- There are the four living creatures, creatures with many eyes and creatures with different purposes, but we don't understand or know what to call them.

- Christ took the place of the high priest's even though the high priest was living at the time of Jesus.

How did Jesus' becoming high priest affect the law and change the course of blood sacrifices?

_____

_____

_____

_____

- When Jesus talked to the high priest, He never mentioned that He would be the new high priest; He just let that happen.

- Jesus was tormented and tortured, and terrible things happened to Him.

- The law was in place at the time Jesus was living, but it was an old broken system.

- The Ark of the Covenant was not in the Holy of Holies. It was considered: *Ichabod,* which means "the glory has departed." The Ark was gone.

- Jesus knew it wasn't there and that the glory had left.

- The Pharisees had a fake religion, and I believe Jesus announced judgment on them.

- They were trying to hide that the glory had departed and that there was no power.

- Jesus was the King from another kingdom that came to earth and walked among us.

- He came to enforce a new agreement and a New Covenant with His blood.

- He handed Himself over and became the sacrificial Lamb.

- God instituted the blood sacrifice from the beginning in the book of Genesis, and now we must look at the sacrifice of Jesus as being the one that met all the requirements.

- Blood has always been required; that's why it was presented once a year in the Holy of Holies.

- The high priest was able to go in and put the blood on the mercy seat between the Cherubim on the gold plate on top of the Ark.

- He was to announce the name of God with that blood, and he wasn't judged.

- He would live through that and do this for the forgiveness of sins for the nation of Israel; then he'd back out of the Holy of Holies (Leviticus 16:8-34).

- Now, Jesus goes in there with His own blood.

How did Jesus meet all the requirements of becoming the high priest?

_____

_____

_____

_____

JESUS THE SACRIFICIAL LAMB

- The book of Hebrews is believed to have be written by Paul, but he was cloaking himself.

- He was writing to the Hebrew people explaining to them all that was done through Jesus Christ.

- Paul encountered the Lord and received revelation for the Gospel.

- He claims that Jesus Christ Himself taught him, and he disappeared for many years (Galatians 1:1-18).

- ❖ **Hebrews 9:11:** "But Christ came as High Priest of the good things to come, with the greater and more perfect tabernacle not made with hands, that is, not of this creation."

  - Paul is saying that the true temple, the true Holy of Holies, and the true Ark of the Covenant, are in heaven: they are not of this creation.

  - As a result of Christ's sacrifice, we no longer need a sacrificed animal every year. His blood was enough.

- Everything has been done, and it's taken care of in the very center of heaven, in the throne room.
- It's where God Himself sits on the mercy seat.
- Jesus' blood is presented there, and the name of God is announced.
- Jesus, the high priest, is the One who does this.
- When you acknowledge Jesus Christ as the sacrificial Lamb, your sins have been taken care of immediately, and your name is written in the Lambs Book of Life (Revelation 13:8).
- You are acknowledged or known when you say, "I accept the only true sacrifice, the Lamb of God; Jesus Christ."
- When you confess with your mouth that Jesus is Lord of your life, and you acknowledge Jesus, you're confessing this before God and the angels, and your sins are completely gone (Romans 10:9).
- Your sins get wiped away at that very moment.

Explain where the blood is today and how your sins have been taken care of?

_____

_____

_____

_____

ETERNAL REDEMPTION

❖ As God instructed Moses on building the tabernacle, God told Moses to ensure it was built accurately, exactly how God gave it to him because they were exact replicas of what is in heaven (Exodus 25:9).

- When you go to the Lord in prayer, remember that your sins are forgiven because of the transaction between God and Moses.
- There is a tabernacle in heaven, and the blood is there because Jesus took His blood with Him into the Holy of Holies.

❖ **Hebrews 9:12:** "Not with the blood of goats and calves, but with His own blood He entered the Most Holy Place once for all, having obtained eternal redemption."

- When it talks about "The blood of goats and calves," it's referring to what God would tell them to do for different sacrifices and grain offerings.
- Everything is perfect now with God, and it has all been satisfied.
- Jesus took care of all the sacrifices that were required up until that time.
- It's called *eternal redemption*.
- The blood of Jesus speaks just like Abel's blood cried out from the ground, and God said to Cain, "I can hear your brother's blood crying out."
- Blood has a voice, and Jesus' blood is speaking, and it's telling the Father that our sins are forgiven!

- As you appear before the Father, the blood is speaking and saying, "This is one of ours, they've been purchased."

- This transaction needs to happen in everyone's life, and that's how you become born again.

- The blood of Jesus is enough.

- He became the perfect sacrifice for humanity.

- Jesus was born as a human being, and He was also God. He was not a hybrid.

- We were born into this world as humans, a part of mankind.

- Those in the Bible who had interbred weren't fully human, and they did not have a resurrection, nor could they obtain redemption (Genesis 6:2).

- Jesus goes to the Father on our behalf to redeem those who are human.

- There is a temptation to hybridize today, and we want to stay fully human so that we can confess Jesus as our savior.

- The blood of bulls and goats cleansed and purified the flesh of sin in the Old Testament, but it wasn't a permanent solution for the sin problem.

- Jesus' bloodshed on the cross was permanent, and His blood speaks forever.

What is the significance of blood as a whole? Why is it so essential to remain a pure stock human?

_____

_____

_____

_____

THE SPOTLESS LAMB

❖ <u>**Hebrews 9:14:**</u> "How much more shall the blood of Christ, who through the eternal Spirit offered Himself without spot to God, cleanse your conscience from dead works to serve the living God?"

DISCUSSION:

Whenever you see spots and blemishes being mentioned in the Bible, it is referring to genetic defects. When you have a pure-bred animal, it has certain features, but if you crossbreed, it's not going to be the full stock of the animal. Do you remember Laban and Jacob? Jacob was working for Laban, and God showed him how to get speckled marks on the livestock. Laban didn't want them; he wanted the purebred because the animals used for sacrifices had to be perfect, which meant they couldn't have these spots. That's where you get the blemishes. The Bible talks about the Bride and the Lamb without spot or wrinkle, the pure stalk animal, the pure, unblemished sacrifice. Even in the time of Jesus, if you brought a lamb that was blemished, it was considered a genetic defect, and it was rejected. The priests would inspect your sacrifice before it was killed, and it couldn't have any blemishes; it says that right in the law. The animals had to be perfect to represent what was coming.

- Jesus was a pure stock human being.
- There were no genetic defects.
- If you trace His bloodline, you'll see that there was nothing wrong with Him, and there were no hybrid races in His bloodline.
- Jesus was without spot or blemish, and the goats presented had none, so there must have been something going on with blood and bloodlines.

- Jesus' blood was so precious because it wasn't tainted in any way.

- His blood washes us away of sin.

- Sin had to do with what happened *in* the garden and *after* the garden.

- God had to destroy the whole earth because they were interbreeding with one other, and it was corrupt, so He had to stop it (Genesis 6:11).

- We are cleansed from dead works, as well as our conscience, to serve the living God, so you don't think about dead works or acts of sin.

- You don't have the desire to sin anymore.

- The blood of Jesus takes care of the sin problem within you.

- Your position with God is also taken care of through the blood of Jesus.

What has the blood of Jesus done for us?

_____

_____

_____

_____

_____

JESUS THE MEDIATOR

❖ **<u>Hebrews 9:15:</u>** And for this reason, He is the Mediator of the new covenant, by means of death, for the redemption of the transgressions under the first covenant, that those who are called may receive the promise of the eternal inheritance.

- Jesus is the mediator of the New Covenant, which means He is a lawyer that looks over between the two parties: God and man.
- When you come into a Covenant, you sign papers of agreement, and He becomes the one to bring the two parties together.
- Jesus did this with the Father and us.
- He was the mediator that sat down at the table and said, "All of this has been fulfilled, and I need each of you to sign here. Here's the agreement, and here's what you each get."
- He entered the position of a mediator through His death.
- He had to die to become the mediator between God and man.
- It's a promise that we receive as an inheritance now.

What does Jesus do as mediator?

_____

_____

_____

_____

CHAPTER TWO

Inheritance and Covenant

For where there is a testament, there must also of necessity be the death of the testator. For a testament is in force after men are dead, since it has no power at all while the testator lives. Therefore not even the first covenant was dedicated without blood. For when Moses had spoken every precept to all the people according to the law, he took the blood of calves and goats, with water, scarlet wool, and hyssop, and sprinkled both the book itself and all the people saying, "This is the blood of the covenant which God has commanded you." Then likewise he sprinkled with blood both the tabernacle and all the vessels of the ministry. And according to the law almost all things are purified with blood, and without shedding of blood there is no remission.

—Hebrews 9:16-22

DISCUSSION:

Jesus, the mediator of the New Covenant, received the promise because He was obedient. We have an inheritance because we are heirs of God and co-heirs with Jesus. Whatever Jesus received, we also receive. Jesus, the Son, received the kingdom, and all the benefits of heaven, not only in this life but in the next life; we share in these benefits with Him. We get to distribute this gift with others by telling them that their sins are forgiven, and they have an inheritance in Christ Jesus because he is our mediator. He is vouching for us and enforcing that the deal goes through correctly. The Holy Spirit is also enforcing the inheritance and the Covenant we have.

WILLS AND TESTAMENTS

❖ **Hebrews 9:16:** "For where there is a testament, there must also of necessity be the death of the testator."

- If someone leaves you a will, it's rare for you to encounter that will until that person passes away.
- When they pass away, then you receive the inheritance because of death.
- In this scripture Paul is saying that in a normal situation, you receive your inheritance when the person passes, and they pass that on to you.
- This testament is a legally binding agreement with a person while they're alive.

- There's a list of all the benefits that will be transferred upon death and to whom it goes.

- Jesus is sitting at a table with the New Covenant. It's based on better promises and a better Covenant.

- He's saying that all these things in heaven are already set apart; they're already Holy.

- This testament is set apart. Christ entered in and took care of all of this for you.

- We don't always understand that with a binding Covenant in heaven, there are delays down here on the manifestation of things.

- That's why we must have faith because faith brings it from the heavenly realm into this realm.

- The High Priest, Jesus, entered in and took care of this, and now we have all the benefits in the New Covenant.

- Jesus only had to do it once, and it's permanent. Forever.

What all did we receive when Jesus died?

_____

_____

_____

_____

THE BLOOD RESOLVED THE ISSUE OF SIN

- Christ took care of your sins, so you wouldn't be able to find that record if you were to go to heaven.

- You won't find sin in heaven. There is no record of it there.

- Jesus bought humanity back, and everything has been cleansed.

- If a person stands before God and their name is not part of the Lamb's Book of Life, it's because they did not acknowledge that Jesus was The Way.

- There's a different judgment for a Christian than a non-Christian.

- As a Christian, you will not be judged with the world if you serve God and do not fall away.

- In the parables and in what Jesus said, you can see that judgment for us is an audit.

- When you appear before the Lord, that final time, it's just to give an account (2 Corinthians 5:10).

- As Christians, we are cleansed of our sins.

- If you have confessed that Jesus is Lord, you've repented of your sins, and you walk in repentance, then your trespasses are forgiven.

- Do not feel guilty any longer.

- Jesus has already paved the way for you to talk to the Father.

- Your position with Him is relational. You're in a relationship; you're not under the law.

- We, as Christians, walk in the light, and we walk in eternal redemption.

- We should be asking ourselves: What did you do with what God gave you?

DISCUSSION:

When I appeared before the Lord, I was aware of what I had been given. I was shown what I did with what I was given. I saw the opportunities I had and how I didn't take advantage of situations and produce more from what was given. That was a hard thing for me. Thank goodness I got to come back. Now I can do much more because I know how it works here on earth. I want to be faithful with what I've been given. I saw that it was about my relationship with Him and how I worked with God. I received rewards for what I did with what I was given. He never addressed sin with me because sin was dealt with. He addressed the times I didn't do what I should've done and didn't take advantage of the situations. I could have had a larger crop if I had been more diligent.

Is God keeping an inventory of your sins? What is He most concerned about with your life here? What does judgment look like for a Christian?

_____

_____

_____

_____

THE LAW AND SACRIFICE VERSUS THE BLOOD OF JESUS

❖ <u>**Hebrews 10:1-4:**</u> "For the law, having a shadow of the good things to come, *and* not the very image of the things, can never with these same sacrifices, which they offer continually year by year, make those who approach perfect. For then would they not have ceased to be offered? For the worshipers, once purified, would have had no more consciousness of sins. But in those *sacrifices there is* a reminder of sins every year. For *it is* not possible that the blood of bulls and goats could take away sins.

- The system in place was not perfect or permanent.
- Sacrifices delayed the judgment of sin.
- Sacrifices were in place until Jesus came.
- God wasn't pleased with the system, so He prepared a body for Jesus to be the perfect sacrifice.

❖ <u>**Hebrews 10:5-10:**</u> Therefore, when He came into the world, He said: "Sacrifice and offering You did not desire, But a body You have prepared for Me. In burnt offerings and *sacrifices* for sin. You had no pleasure. Then I said, 'Behold, I have come— In the volume of the book it is written of Me— To do Your will, O God.'" Previously saying, "Sacrifice and offering, burnt offerings, and *offerings* for sin You did not desire, nor had pleasure *in them*" (which are offered according to the law), then He said, "Behold, I have come to do Your will, O God." He takes away the first that He may establish the second. By that will we have been sanctified through the offering of the body of Jesus Christ once *for all.*

- Jesus came to fix everything, and He made the old system look ineffective.

- You can see how ineffective it was by the way Jesus came against the Pharisees.

- They were constantly reminding people of their sins instead of helping them.

- They were making the law so hard on people there was no hope for them.

- With the old system and sacrifice in place, there was always a reminder of sin.

- Had sacrifice worked, then there would be no consciousness of sin, and it would've been a permanent solution, but it was not.

- Now that sacrifices are done away with, we have a New Covenant through Jesus, and the veil in the temple is rent or torn.

- When Jesus was crucified, He said, "It is finished," and the veil was rent.

- Now, the Holy of Holies is open to us because of Jesus' blood shed for the remission of sin.

- He is the New and Living Way.

- He took away the first to establish the second. He came and transferred everything over to the new.

- Jesus came with the Good News, and He announced it to everyone. That is how we should be in our faith.

- We're going into the New Covenant with the Father God.

Explain why the old way was so ineffective? How is Jesus' New and Living way more effective?

_____

_____

_____

_____

❖ **Hebrews 10:12-18:** "But this Man, after He had offered one sacrifice for sins forever, sat down at the right hand of God, from that time waiting till His enemies are made His footstool. For by one offering, He has perfected forever those who are being sanctified. But the Holy Spirit also witnesses to us; for after He had said before, "This *is* the covenant that I will make with them after those days, says the Lord: I will put My laws into their hearts, and in their minds I will write them," *then He adds,* "Their sins and their lawless deeds I will remember no more." And where these have been forgiven, sacrifice for sin is no longer necessary."

- Jesus is seated at the right hand of God, and He's waiting for His enemies are made His footstool. This is once and forever.
- People are still asking God to do certain things He's already done.
- God has done everything He's going to do about satan. He has already judged him.
- Jesus isn't going to do another thing about the devil because He has already completed everything.
- He gave us His name. He gave us His blood. He gave us the keys.

THE PRECIOUS BLOOD OF JESUS

- The church is supposed to be enforcing this process that Jesus went through and established.

- The church is supposed to rise up with the keys of authority in the kingdom through the name and blood of Jesus.

- We, as the church, are to bring the enemy. We're supposed to conquer the enemy on earth and bring his head to the feet of Jesus for Him to rest His feet.

- What they did in the days of kings was they would bring the head of the defeated one to the feet of the king for him to put his feet on to show his authority that he had conquered him.

What are we as the church supposed to be doing in this time?

_____

_____

_____

_____

- Jesus has become everything we need.

- When He left the earth and sat at the right hand of God, He sent another one like Him, the Holy Spirit (John 14:16 and John 16:7).

- We're perfected in our position in Christ but were in a broken world, so the Holy Spirit is needed to enforce the covenant and enforce the blessing.

- The Holy Spirit is our advocate, lawyer, and mediator.

- He's the one who communicates our benefits to us.

- He tells us what to implement in our lives and guides us, but it won't get done if we don't do it.

DR. KEVIN L. ZADAI

- We need to pray. God knows what we're going through, but we still must pray because a transaction must happen.

- Jesus came and did all He's going to do, and He gave it all to us.

- Through the Holy Spirit in us, that transfer must happen.

- There must be a manifestation through that transfer and transaction.

- We're being perfected as we walk it out, but we're perfected in position.

- Your conscience has been cleansed, and you should not even want to sin.

- If you sin, it's an indication you may need deliverance, and you need further to understand the knowledge and wisdom of the covenant.

- As believers, we need to understand what we have in Jesus Christ.

- People that don't understand what they have are in a battle all the time.

- We're perfected through the blood of Jesus.

- We have a mediator that implements the New Covenant, and we're perfected through that.

- The Holy Spirit is our mediator here on the earth because He is with us now. Jesus is our mediator in heaven.

THE NEW COVENANT

- The Holy Spirit is the one who witnesses the New Covenant in us.

- The Holy Spirit testifies and enforces this inheritance.

- We need to go from positional to relational with God.

- The relational part of the blood continually cleanses us of dead works and its consciousness in our mind.

- This is where we need to walk in the benefits.

- The devil fights us because he can't keep people from getting saved, so he tries to keep us as baby Christians.

- Baby Christians understand the positional, but they don't understand the relational because it wasn't taught.

- The devil tries to keep us from walking in the benefits of our salvation.

- Looking to our earlier scripture, Hebrews 10:16 says, "In the New Covenant, that the Lord is going to write the laws on our hearts and minds."

- The Holy Spirit engraves the Word of God within us, and He's able to renew our minds through that Word.

- It's not just the born-again experience; there's the renewing of the mind that takes place as well.

- Then, there's the crucifixion of the flesh and walking in the crucified life.

- Our sins and lawless deeds He will remember no more.

- Positionally, everything is taken care of.

- It's the fruit He is looking for in us. That is why Jesus said, "Produce fruit in keeping with repentance" (Matthew3:8).

- There's no remission of sin without blood. Jesus took care of this for us.

What does the Holy Spirit do?

_____

_____

_____

_____

THE ASSURANCE OF OUR FAITH

❖ **Hebrews 10:19-23:** "Therefore, brethren, having boldness to enter the Holiest by the blood of Jesus, by a new and living way which He consecrated for us, through the veil, that is, His flesh, and *having* a High Priest over the house of God,"

DISCUSSION:

Prior to Christ, high priests were afraid that if anything wasn't right, or if they didn't do something right, they would be struck dead in the Holy of Holies. They would tie a rope to one of their ankles so that if they died, no one else could go in there after them because they would die also. The rope attached to them was there so that if anything happened, they could just pull their dead body out by the rope. Now, we are called to enter boldly into the Holy of Holies, not just humbly on our knees. You don't have a sin consciousness anymore, so you can enter boldly. That is the message we were given at the end of the age.

- The only way to have boldness is to know you are cleansed and that you're in right standing.
- The High Priests would tiptoe into the Holy of Holies because they weren't sure if they did everything right.
- Boldness is when, you are sure.
- Jesus did it right in the flesh, and He broke through that veil for us.
- Now we can do that. We can break through the veil of the flesh.
- The veil symbolized the flesh that separated the Holy place from the Holy of Holies.
- We can enter that now because it's been rent.

Why and how are we able to enter the Holy place with boldness?

_____

_____

_____

_____

❖ Every day I think about drawing near to God with a true heart that has full assurance in faith. I build my faith up by praying in the Holy Spirit, and I have a true heart because I stay in the love of God. My heart is sprinkled from an evil conscience. I'm made perfect in my spirit, and the evil conscience is also cleansed in my mind. The Father has covered all three parts: the spirit, mind, and body. People can have heart and soul and have feelings, but it's hard to discern if it's spiritual or soulish. The word of God is the only one that can separate that. (Hebrews 4:12).

- The heart can be attached to feelings, and it can be attached to thoughts.
- The soul is made up of the mind, will, and emotions.
- They're not able to be separated by you.
- The Word of God is the only one that can separate them (Hebrews 4:12).
- Even your heart can have feelings and thoughts coming from your soul.
- Only the Word of God can tell the difference between the soul and the spirit.
- That's how intricately interwoven they are.

❖ **Hebrews 10:22-23:** "let us draw near with a true heart in full assurance of faith, having our hearts sprinkled from an evil conscience and our bodies washed with pure water. Let us hold fast the confession of *our* hope without wavering, for He who promised *is* faithful."

- As a Christian matures, their conscience will not be evil, it's going to be cleansed, and your heart is going to be pure.
- Your body is going to be washed with pure water.
- If you wash your body and your mind every day with the Word, and you feed your heart with the Word, then all three will start to work together.

What do you think the result will be if your soul is not renewed? What do we do to cleanse our souls?

_____

_____

_____

_____

_____

_____

CHAPTER THREE

There is Life in the Blood

But you shall not eat flesh with its life, that is, its blood. Surely for your lifeblood, I will demand a reckoning; from the hand of every beast I will require it, and from the hand of man. From the hand of every man's brother I will require the life of man. "Whoever sheds man's blood, By man his blood shall be shed; For in the image of God He made man. And as for you, be fruitful and multiply; Bring forth abundantly in the earth And multiply in it."

—Genesis 9:4-7

DISCUSSION:

If a man's blood is shed, God will require blood in return. You cannot kill another man because God will require your blood. That's because God made man in His image. If you have murdered or killed someone, you can be forgiven. If you're a Christian, you are forgiven of every sin. When scripture refers to the blood, it has to do with the image of God. When you look at Adam, he was taken from the ground, and God breathed life into him, and he became a living soul. He had blood in him. That's why God said there is life in the blood (Leviticus 17:11). That's why you don't drink blood or kill other human beings; it's because we don't have the authority to do that.

- We have death, people being killed, and war in a broken and fallen world.
- We have all of this, but it's not the perfect will of God.
- You can't shed another man's blood because God made man in His image.
- No one has the authority to kill or murder anyone.
- Pilate didn't have the authority to kill Jesus, and neither did Cain have the authority to kill Abel, but he did.

❖ **Matthew 27:22-23:** "Pilate said to them, "What then shall I do with Jesus who is called Christ?" *They* all said to him, "Let Him be crucified!" Then the governor said, "Why, what evil has He done?" But they cried out all the more, saying, "Let Him be crucified!"

- The people were saying to crucify Jesus.
- Pilate asked, "Why? What evil has He done?" In other words, if this is going to be punishment, I need to know why?"
- The people cried out more for Him to be crucified.
- At that point, He would be killed innocently without reason, just like Cain innocently killed Abel.

❖ <u>**Matthew 27:24-25:**</u> "When Pilate saw that he could not prevail at all, but rather *that* a tumult was rising, he took water and washed *his* hands before the multitude, saying, "I am innocent of the blood of this just Person. You see *to it.*" And all the people answered and said, "His blood *be* on us and on our children."

- Pilate washed his hands and claimed his innocence.

- According to Roman law, you can't kill someone who is not guilty.

- He announced Jesus' innocence and didn't want anything to do with it.

- In Genesis 4:6-7, God came to Cain and said, *"Why are you so angry?" "Why do you look so dejected? You will be accepted if you do what is right. But if you refuse to do what is right, then watch out! Sin is crouching at the door, eager to control you. But you must subdue it and be its master."*

- It would've been taken care of if Cain had offered a blood sacrifice because sin required a blood payment.

- The sin that crouched at the door is like a crouching lion that desires to have you for prey.

- Sin is like an animal that desires its prey and its way.

- The sin was crouching at the door of Cain's heart, desiring to have him.

- When Pilate washed his hands of the situation concerning Jesus, and he didn't take it on, it had to be transferred to someone else.

- Pilate was essentially saying that the Roman government would have nothing to do with Jesus' death. It went right back to the Pharisees and the people who brought Jesus there.

- For the responsibility to come upon the people, they had to verbalize it and take ownership of it.

- When the crowd answered Pilate in Verse 25 and said, "His blood be on us and on our children," they invited a curse upon themselves, and they included their children in it. They brought it upon themselves.

According to Matthew 27:24-25, why did Pilate wash his hands of the situation concerning Jesus, and what did he do?

_____

_____

_____

_____

- ❖ **Matthew 27:26:** "Then he released Barabbas to them; and when he had scourged Jesus, he delivered *Him* to be crucified.

  - The people wanted Barabbas back.

  - He was an insurrectionist and was already thrown in jail for an uprising.

  - They took this criminal back, and he was set free.

  - The shedding of blood requires payment.

  - Sin requires the shedding of blood.

  - If sin is not taken care of, it will require blood, and there will be repercussions.

  - When you forgive, you're forgiven. When you give, you receive.

  - It's part of how it works in this realm because the realms are broken.

  - So, we need to circumvent the sin problem in the fallen world.

  - You're taken care of by the blood.

  - There are all kinds of broken covenants and broken things going on here.

- The people asked for the curse and the blood to be upon them; they didn't discern what God was doing.
- It was demonically inspired for those people to say what they did.

JESUS, THE BREAD OF LIFE

❖ **John 6:47-51:** "Most assuredly, I say to you, he who believes in Me has everlasting life. I am the bread of life. Your fathers ate the manna in the wilderness, and are dead. This is the bread which comes down from heaven, that one may eat of it and not die. I am the living bread which came down from heaven. If anyone eats of this bread, he will live forever; and the bread that I shall give is My flesh, which I shall give for the life of the world."

- When Jesus announced that He is the bread of life, He was saying, "It's not just by listening to my teachings, it's taking me in, where there's a change."
- Jesus wanted to go deeper with them on a relational level.
- He knew they were just following Him around to see the miracles and because they were being fed.
- He wanted to show them that He was the bread that came down from heaven, just like the supernatural manna that came in the wilderness.

❖ <u>**John 6:47-58:**</u> "The Jews therefore quarreled among themselves, saying, "How can this Man give us *His* flesh to eat?" Then Jesus said to them, "Most assuredly, I say to you, unless you eat the flesh of the Son of Man and drink His blood, you have no life in you. Whoever eats My flesh and drinks My blood has eternal life, and I will raise him up at the last day. For My flesh is food indeed, and My blood is drink indeed. He who eats My flesh and drinks My blood abides in Me, and I in him.

- He was trying to get them to go to a different level, a higher level of understanding.
- As you go deeper, there's a point where people can't go on for whatever reason. It's not always for the right reasons that they leave.
- People left Jesus, and there was hardly anyone left.
- He was taking them to a deeper level of understanding with relationship, transformation, and change.
- He didn't want them hearing all the time and not being changed by the words.

❖ <u>**John 6:57-58:**</u> "As the living Father sent Me, and I live because of the Father, so he who feeds on Me will live because of Me. This is the bread which came down from heaven—not as your fathers ate the manna, and are dead. He who eats this bread will live forever."

- They received Manna every day, but it didn't cause them to live forever.
- He explained to them that when you eat of Him, the substance of who He is will give you eternal life.

- The bread that comes down from heaven, if one eats of it, they'll never die.

- He started to speak on eternal life and spiritual things, and when you do that, it separates the sheep from the goats.

- When hardship comes, people start to lose faith and fall away. You begin to see a separation, and who was there the whole time with the Lord or not.

- When this happens, I can see a character change in the way people act.

- You can't say, "They changed," because maybe they were that way the whole time.

- Times of testing and hardship reveal where people are.

- I think that's what Jesus was doing here.

- He realizes that the temperature needs to be turned up with the people following Him, and there were thousands of people following Him.

What would the people receive if they believed in Him?

_____

_____

_____

_____

DISCUSSION:

Jesus talked to the people and showed them the symbolism throughout the Old Testament, revealing that He was the fulfillment. He could show them that He was, but they were not very understanding. He had to explain things in-depth. Even the disciples weren't getting it, and they would pull Him aside to get clarification. Every time Jesus would speak, it would cause a problem. Many left Him when He spoke about eating His flesh and drinking His blood. Some passages say that *everyone* left Him that day. He asked the disciples if they would leave Him, and Peter answered Jesus and said, "Where would we go? You have the words of life" (John 6:68). They had left their jobs and everything to follow Him for three years. They knew He was the Messiah.

What was Jesus trying to convey to the people by saying He was the bread of life?

_____

_____

_____

_____

SPIRITUAL FOOD AND EATING THE WORD OF LIFE

- We need to eat from the Word of God.
- Even if it's one word you pick up from the Bible every day, concentrate on that word, look it up, and discover the meaning.
- Eat the word as though it's a loaf of bread.
- Eat slices of bread every day.

- Eat one word at a time and meditate on it.

- Let the Holy Spirit show you and bring life to that word.

- He is the living Word.

- He is the slice of bread that came down from heaven.

- He is going to give you slices. He's going to give you a whole loaf.

- Whatever you need, there's never going to be an end to it. You're never going to have too much.

- You will always have more than you need to eat.

- You're going to be changed by it.

- You take in Jesus' flesh by taking His spiritual body and His spiritual blood.

- His blood went to heaven, so there had to be some sort of transference from one to the other.

- The people who left Jesus couldn't transfer over to the spiritual part.

- Fleshly people do not make the cut.

- The physical realm is a replica of the spiritual realm.

- We're in a fallen world, but everything is patterned after heaven.

- There are things in heaven that you'll see down here, but in heaven, they're at a higher level because the system in heaven isn't broken.

What is the key to staying out of the flesh and remaining in Jesus?

_____

_____

_____

_____

❖ When the people started arguing amongst themselves, saying, "How can this man give us His flesh to eat?" They were caught up in the natural definitions and didn't realize what was happening spiritually.

- As you hear the Word, something spiritual happens to your body.

- Transformation takes place because the words of the Spirit are going out, and when you partake of the Word of God, it becomes part of you.

- Then when you give it out to others, it just keeps multiplying.

- It's how the physical and spiritual go back and forth from one realm to the other.

- Jesus said, "If you don't eat my flesh and you don't drink my blood, you have no life in you" (John 6:53).

- He was saying that we have to partake of Him spiritually.

- The people were looking to the flesh. That's what we call carnal Christians or people of the world. You can't always tell until things start happening, and they begin to unravel.

- You start to see who they are.

- There are sheep and goats, and God will separate them.

- There are tares, and there is wheat. God will separate them.

- There are the wise virgins and the unwise virgins. God will separate them.

- It starts to become evident if you look at the situation.

- You will begin to see when people don't make the jump from the natural to the supernatural.

- Jesus was essentially saying, "If you don't do this, you'll have no part of me, and if you do this, you will be risen in the resurrection on the last day, for my flesh is food, indeed. My blood is drink, indeed."
- You're going to manifest in this life what you eat. You will live forever.
- The Word of God feeds your spirit, cleanses your mind, and helps your body.

❖ There's a transference from the spiritual power that rose Jesus from the dead, it dwells in you and will quicken your mortal body (Romans 8:11). It makes contact from the spiritual to the physical and affects your body. Jesus was telling the people that it is not just His physical blood; we are drinking of His lifeblood. He wants us to shift over to this understanding.

What does Jesus require of us in reference to His flesh and blood?

_____

_____

_____

_____

CHAPTER FOUR

The Blood Makes You Righteous

*For He made Him who knew no sin to be sin for us, that we
might become the righteousness of God in Him.*
—*2 Corinthians 5:21*

DISCUSSION:

Jesus was the perfect man; His body and blood were perfect. He was the perfect
sacrifice for our condition of sin. Not only did Jesus conquer sin, but He defeated
the demonic, and He did so in their genetics and bloodlines. That is why the blood
is essential, and we need to understand it more in-depth. The blood of Jesus is related
to righteousness and our position. Church people are not always knowledgeable of
kingdom authority and power. That's where the fivefold ministry of the church
comes in, and teachers must educate everyone on these things. For Christians, it's
not just about your position but your relationship with God and Jesus that gives you
the authority to operate in the kingdom. That's why the seven sons of Sceva couldn't

cast the devil out (Acts 19:11-20). The seven sons said, "I cast you out in the name of Jesus that Paul preaches," The demons resplied and said, "I know Jesus, and I know Paul, but who are you?" The demons didn't listen to them, and instead, they beat them up. We can see it's not just about our position; it's also about our relationship with Him. The demons listened to the seventy-two that were sent out (Luke 10:1-20). We don't know the kind of instruction they received except for what's written, but there had to be some type of relationship between them and Jesus.

❖ **<u>Romans 3:21-23:</u>** "But now the righteousness of God apart from the law is revealed, being witnessed by the Law and the Prophets, even the righteousness of God, through faith in Jesus Christ, to all and on all who believe. For there is no difference; for all have sinned and fall short of the glory of God,

- Everyone has sinned and fallen short. The blood was enough for everyone.
- We've all been redeemed, and the price was paid, but not everyone goes to heaven.
- You fell short, but Jesus Christ is the way, and He made a way for you.
- The gospel is announcing that the price has been paid.
- Receive Jesus. Announce Him with your lips, believe in your heart that Jesus is Lord, and you shall be saved.
- You will inherit everlasting life and not go to hell.

THE PRECIOUS BLOOD OF JESUS

How were we justified for our sins and falling short of the glory of God?

_____

_____

_____

❖ <u>**Romans 3:24-26**</u> "being justified freely by His grace through the redemption that is in Christ Jesus, whom God set forth _as_ a propitiation by His blood, through faith, to demonstrate His righteousness, because in His forbearance God had passed over the sins that were previously committed, to demonstrate at the present time His righteousness, that He might be just and the justifier of the one who has faith in Jesus."

- Being justified was by the grace of God through redemption.
- That's why we have to announce it to demons; they know that we're justified.
- The blood was enough for everyone; that's why we announce and acknowledge Jesus Christ.
- The demons want to keep people out of that, so they get people not to confess their sins or to accept Jesus.
- If people do that, they stay as immature baby Christians for the rest of their lives.
- Demons know they can't stop Christians from maturing, so they try to get them to be offended.
- They work in different ways to slow Christians down so that they don't go into the Holy of Holies boldly because they are in offense.
- There are different stages of how the devil deals with people, but the bottom line is that blood is powerful enough to make a person righteous.

- The blood is powerful enough to defeat the devil.

- The devil strategizes against individual Christians to keep them from being effective.

- If the enemy can't stop a person from getting saved, he tries to make them ineffective by lying about the gospel.

- It's not enough to just get people saved. Jesus said, "Go forth and make disciples of all nations" (Matthew 28:19-20). He didn't say, go out and make converts, even though that's what we do.

- A disciple adheres and follows the teachings of Jesus the Messiah.

- What a disciple does is follow the Rabbi and adhere to his disciplines.

- The Disciples followed Jesus around and called Him Rabbi.

- Disciples are known as disciplines.

How powerful is the blood of Jesus, and what does it do?

_____

_____

_____

_____

Explain what a disciple of Jesus does.

_____

_____

_____

_____

YOUR RECORD IN HEAVEN

- Because of the blood of Jesus, your sins are forgiven. They are completely wiped away and transferred to Jesus.

- Jesus became the substitution so that sin doesn't show on your record.

- That's why the demons are so flipped out about the blood of Jesus.

- They don't want a person claiming the blood because they're defeated and ineffective in anything they do.

- The name of Jesus is a legal transaction.

- When you announce the name of Jesus, you are displaying authority and God's ownership.

- The blood of Jesus is related to your relationship to the Father God.

- If you acknowledge the blood of Jesus, then your sin problem has been taken care of.

- You become righteous, and that righteousness is demonstrated because Jesus took your record of sin upon Himself.

- He transferred over His righteousness and His right standing, so when you pull up your record in heaven, it will be the record of Jesus.

- It won't be your life's record of sin.

How is there no record of our sin in Heaven?

_____

_____

_____

_____

RIGHTEOUSNESS AND FAITH

- His righteousness is passed on to you, and He no longer sees your sin. It doesn't exist. It's gone. He did everything right.

- Jesus demonstrated His righteousness by taking your sin.

- Through faith in Jesus, you are justified!

- Abraham was justified by faith. He didn't have the law to obey, and his faith caused him to do the right thing.

- We are justified by faith in Jesus Christ.

- We inherit His good record and how He did things.

- The blood of Jesus caused righteousness to come.

- We are to live a righteous life.

- We are to announce to others that they can live a righteous life, be made righteous, and not talk about sinful nature.

- The spirit of this world wants to keep people trapped; it doesn't want to propagate good things because people might get set free.

- If the blood of Jesus has justified a person, they have to decide to accept righteousness.

- If they are non-Christian, they need to accept Jesus. If they are a Christian, they need to accept the justification.

- We need to discern that through the blood of Jesus, we've been made righteous. Then, we need to manifest it and walk it out.

- Jesus walked the righteous life out.

- In heaven, you will see that you inherited His status.

- You inherited the way He walked so that you can walk as Jesus did.

- You can be imitators of God as dearly loved children (Ephesians 5:1).

How is it that we are Justified?

_____

_____

_____

_____

How do you walk as a dearly loved child of God?

_____

_____

_____

_____

❖ <u>**Romans 5:6-11**</u>: "For when we were still without strength, in due time Christ died for the ungodly. For scarcely for a righteous man will one die; yet perhaps for a good man someone would even dare to die. But God demonstrates His own love toward us in that while we were still sinners, Christ died for us. Much more then, having now been justified by His blood, we shall be saved from wrath through Him. For if when we were enemies we were reconciled to God through the death of His Son, much more, having been reconciled, we shall be saved by His life. And not only _that,_ but we also rejoice in God through our Lord Jesus Christ, through whom we have now received the reconciliation.

DISCUSSION:

We have to learn to let the Holy Spirit live His life out through us. It's not about status. This verse in Romans says, "For when we were still without strength in due time, Christ died for the ungodly." That's Salvation! The fact is that He died for sinners, not just good people. He died for people that couldn't pay Him back and for people that couldn't be good. This verse is saying that a man might die for his friend or for a righteous person, but God demonstrated His love for us, that while we were in a sinful state, He sent His son.

- He loved us that much, so how much more should we be concentrating on that we are justified by His blood.

- The verse says that we shall be saved from the wrath through Him. In other words, while we are here on this earth, we should be saved from wrath.

- Several verses indicate that we are not appointed to God's wrath.

- Certain judgments will come upon the earth that we're not going to be part of.

- There's a certain point where God will extract us because we're not appointed to wrath.

- We've been saved from the wrath of God through the blood.

- We were enemies, but we were reconciled. How much more should His life save us?

- There should be life flowing through us, where people see that we're saved.

- Salvation includes joining Christ in heaven, but we are supposed to be experiencing salvation is in every area of our lives.

- Now that we receive salvation and walk in it, it should overcome us. We should be encountering Jesus' life in abundance because He's given us life more abundantly (John 10:10).

- If we have been justified, we should no longer feel guilty. Your sins have been forgiven from your past, what you did just yesterday and today. Just repent.

- You're going to do everything right and still feel like you've done something wrong because of the spirit of this world.

- People need to be set free of the guilty conscience because they've been justified; it makes it as though they have never sinned.

- There is no accusing voice against you (Romans 8:1). There is no case against you, and your file has been destroyed.

- Prosperity to me is waking up guilt-free, going to bed guilt-free, and knowing that the blood was enough.

- The demons do not want you to know this, nor do they want you to teach it.

What mindset shift does this verse require from us? How can we share this with others?

_____

_____

_____

_____

_____

_____

_____

_____

CHAPTER FIVE

Partakers of God's Inheritance

*I pray that the eyes of your heart may be enlightened in order that you
may know the hope to which he has called you, the riches of his
glorious inheritance in his holy people.*
—*Ephesians 1:18*

DISCUSSION:

When Paul was sent to Ephesus, it was steeped in witchcraft. At the time, it was one of the capitals of witchcraft. Many people repented, turning in their spell books and burning them (Acts 19:19-20). The Lord moved mightily through Paul there. In the Book of Ephesians, there are powerful insights about spiritual warfare that will advance you in understanding the blood of Jesus. These understandings will help you to eliminate a lot of warfare. You want to be so well equipped that the demons will opt out and not go there with you. You must become educated so that you can teach these skills to the body of Christ so that we can eliminate the demon's ability to engage with us. If the demons feel like you are more powerful, they will leave. In the story of *the seven sons of Sceva*, we saw how they didn't have the authority or power to drive out demons. The demons were determined to take over the seven and run them off, and they succeeded in doing this. You, however, will be well equipped to defeat them.

❖ **Ephesians 1:3-6:** "Blessed be the God and Father of our Lord Jesus Christ, who has blessed us with every spiritual blessing in the heavenly places in Christ, just as He chose us in Him before the foundation of the world, that we should be holy and without blame before Him in love, having predestined us to adoption as sons by Jesus Christ to Himself, according to the good pleasure of His will, to the praise of the glory of His grace, by which He made us accepted in the Beloved.

- "Before creation, He chose us in Him."
- It's not saying He makes some people saved and then others not saved. That's Calvinism.
- It's predestination, as in having foreknowledge.
- It's God knowing the process that needs to happen.
- We were predestined to adoption.
- God is going to adopt you. He will come in, buy you and take you as His own.
- satan wants everyone to feel rejected, guilty, and not deserving of love.
- That's what is infiltrating into the Church.
- In religious circles, people feel like they never quite live up to or ever reach approval. That's the religious mindset working.
- God is saying, I predestined you to be adopted, and you're mine.
- You are not rejected.
- God did this through Jesus Christ to bring people back to Himself.

- According to His good pleasure and will, the blood brought people back to God Himself through Jesus Christ. He wanted to do this.
- God didn't have to do any of this when man sinned. That could have been it, and we would have never known.

How have we been made accepted by God?

_____

_____

_____

_____

❖ **Ephesians 1:7-12** "In Him we have redemption through His blood, the forgiveness of sins, according to the riches of His grace which He made to abound toward us in all wisdom and prudence, having made known to us the mystery of His will, according to His good pleasure which He purposed in Himself, that in the dispensation of the fullness of the times He might gather together in one all things in Christ, both which are in heaven and which are on earth—in Him. In Him also we have obtained an inheritance, being predestined according to the purpose of Him who works all things according to the counsel of His will, that we who first trusted in Christ should be to the praise of His glory.

- God wanted redemption, and many generations have come after Adam and Eve.
- That redemption came through Jesus' blood because His blood causes the forgiveness of sins.
- It's going to be paid out of His riches in His grace.

- He's already taken care of it.

- It was according to His good pleasure. He enjoys doing this, and it's His will.

- His glory and grace are how He made us accepted in the beloved.

- The beloved is the whole body of Christ, the entire family.

How are we to be when we go before the Lord? How did that come to be?

_____

_____

_____

_____

IN ONENESS WITH THE FATHER

DISCUSSION:

We have our spiritual blessings because of the blood of Jesus. The blood of Jesus placed at the mercy seat in heaven caused all these things to be accessed. The blood that's being placed there is both physical and spiritual. People don't understand this, but both realms can work together simultaneously; however, we're not taught how this works. Jesus was raised from the dead. He taught for forty days near Jerusalem, and no one stopped Him. The Roman soldiers knew Jesus was alive. Pilate and Cesare had to know He was alive, yet no one stopped Him for forty days. He would show up and eat actual food with people. He had a physical body and would walk through walls, and the food would go with Him. It wouldn't stay on the wall. These were the two realms being demonstrated, and it's the case with us today. We don't understand how the physical and spiritual can work together. We don't understand that an angel can come and look like a person. He doesn't have a physical body, but he appears to have one. He can eat, pull a sword, and cut something, yet he can disappear and walk through a wall. We need to understand these realms to operate in all God has given us.

- In Ephesus, Paul dealt with carnal Christians who were caught up in the flesh. He considered them babies in Christ.

- They appeared to be spiritual, but they couldn't operate in both the physical realm and the spiritual at the same time.

- They were being used in the spirit, but at the same time, they were doing all these terrible fleshly things.

- They didn't have a handle on how to live in both realms.

- Paul explains to the Ephesians that we're blessed with every spiritual blessing in the heavenly places in Christ.

- Jesus came physically to obtain that for us.

- The crossover is that Jesus did it for us, and we are to adhere and eat of Him.

- We are to eat of His Word and eat of the Spirit.

- When we do this, it causes physical change, even though it's a spiritual thing.

- We manifest the Son of God in our lives by eating spiritual food and yielding to the Holy Spirit in us.

- He is a spirit, but He manifests in the flesh through us.

- Angels can appear physically at any moment, and they can do that at will. You can't explain that.

- The blood of Jesus is very powerful, and it influences you every day.

- You don't see it because it's a spiritual thing, but it should manifest physically.

What causes us to live our lives in unison with both realms?

_____

_____

_____

_____

HE CHOSE US IN HIM

- Why do you think evil spirits manifest through people? It's in their spirits. Evil spirits can physically manifest in someone's body and through their voice because there is a crossover. When the Holy Spirit has your tongue, He's going to talk through you. If the Holy Spirit has your body, He's going to live through you. There's a transference. The body of Christ doesn't understand that the enemy has gotten in, but they should. It's warfare.

  - The plan is to be bought and be holy, without blame, and in perfect love, which explains who you are in Christ.
  - You're in perfect love, you're in holiness, and you're without blame.
  - You are completely justified, and this was all decided before the foundation of the world.
  - God made it available to everyone, but some people never find Him, and they go to hell.

Explain how God has given us a choice to choose Him, yet He already chose us?

_____

_____

_____

_____

❖ In heaven, I saw everyone gathered. All the people that had ever lived that will ever live had been redeemed and made it to heaven. They were all there. I heard the song being sung to the Lamb, and it was beautiful. I realized that the plan had worked. Many people were there. It was planned before the earth was formed and before the foundations of the world.

According to Ephesians 1, explain what God has done for us?

_____

_____

_____

_____

- Jesus causes His grace to abound toward us, which means He expands it out toward us.
- When you hear a gospel message or the Word of God, you should sense that it's abounding, going forth, and prevailing strongly.
- We will also have the understanding and wisdom that comes with it, and it's ever-increasing.
- We should be seeing this happen, and we need to teach others and be like Jesus to make disciples.

- Wisdom causes you to embrace what is coming toward you.

- Prudence causes you to realize what you have, where you count the cost and become a good steward of it.

- The end result in this dispensation and fullness of time is we're all going to be together as one.

- The blood has not only bought us, but at the end of all things, we will be one in Christ, in heaven, and on the earth.

- That's revealing that He will bring the two realms together as one.

❖ We are going to all be together as one. Those who have gone before us are cheering for us. They want us to build upon what they did, not redo what they've done. They want us to go even further. With them, we all accomplish God's purpose and plan. That was the plan. It's not that we just hear the gospel and hold on until He comes, or we pass away. We are to increase and abound in that knowledge and prudence, where it causes an increase in the next generation. We are not just sustaining. When we're at the end of the age, and everyone in heaven and earth has been purchased, we're all together standing as one; it is the summation of the plan of God at that very moment.

What are we to do for the next generation?

_____

_____

_____

_____

- God planned to purchase humanity before He ever formed the earth because the plan was already made.

- Before the foundation of the world, we were already predestined to be in Him.

- The summation of God's plan had to do with blood. It had to do with a purchase before man even sinned.

- satan never had a chance because God had already planned this before man was ever made.

- It is also why satan was defeated.

- If he had known, he would not have crucified the Lord of glory.

- He didn't know the plan. Jesus taught this to Paul.

- "In Him, we've obtained an inheritance, being predestined according to His purpose because He works all things according to the counsel of His will" (Ephesians 1:11).

- "The counsel of His will" means that the Godhead met together, determined their will, and then they created the earth, and they made man.

- It was all predestined according to His purpose from that counsel that they had.

- What we are to do is trust God that it's going to all be wrapped up.

- The purchase that happened through Jesus Christ was the plan from the beginning.

- When you use the name of Jesus, or you invoke the blood, or you mention the blood of Jesus, the reason why it has so many implications in the spirit realm is that it's the very thing that defeated the enemy before there was even a problem.

- When we mention the blood, it's a reminder that God already had planned to defeat the devil before he was the devil and before he ever fell.
- God had already planned this in His foreknowledge, and it's a sore spot with the enemy.

What is the purpose of God's plan at the end?

_____

_____

_____

_____

- ❖ **Colossians 1:9-11:** "For this reason, we also, since the day we heard it, do not cease to pray for you, and to ask that you may be filled with the knowledge of His will in all wisdom and spiritual understanding; that you may walk worthy of the Lord, fully pleasing *Him,* being fruitful in every good work and increasing in the knowledge of God; strengthened with all might, according to His glorious power, for all patience and long-suffering with joy;

  - Paul tells us to be filled with knowledge, wisdom, and spiritual understanding to help us walk worthy of the Lord.
  - The knowledge you have is not meant to be recited; you have it to give you spiritual understanding that causes you to walk it out in the natural realm.
  - You might be pleasing in your position with God, but we want to walk out our relationship with Him by pleasing Him and producing fruit in keeping with repentance (Matthew 3:8).

- Are we pleasing in our relationship with Him?

- There has to be a manifestation.

- Paul uses the word "fruitful." Are we producing fruit in every good work?

- Works aren't eliminated. There are acts of righteousness, fruits of righteousness, and an increase in understanding so people can see it.

- Our lives are a witness of the Lord Jesus Christ, not just our words.

- We are to be strengthened and increase in the glorious power of the Lord.

- We are to increase in patience and long-suffering.

- We are to be partakers of the inheritance.

- We are to unwrap all these beautiful presents that the Lord Jesus obtained for us and partake of them.

- We are to manifest them with the power and strength of the Lord.

- Paul made sure that people understood it was not just the blood of Jesus, positional righteousness, and justice in a person's life, but it was the manifestation in the way they lived.

- It's all part of the power of the blood of Jesus.

According to Colossians 1:9-11, how should our lives reflect our relationship with God?

_____

_____

_____

_____

DR. KEVIN L. ZADAI

CHAPTER SIX

Holy & Blameless

For he chose us in him before the creation of the world to be
holy and blameless in his sight. In love.
—Ephesians 1:4 NIV

DISCUSSION:

We can learn a lot from Paul in Ephesians and Colossians about what the blood of Jesus did for us and the inheritances we have in Christ. It's one thing to receive Jesus and be saved, but it's another thing to be *in* Him and walk *in* our salvation. As Christians, we want our lives to demonstrate our relationship with the Lord and how closely we walk with Him. We want to walk worthy of the Lord, fully pleasing Him, being fruitful in every good work, and increasing in the knowledge of God (Colossians 1:10).

❖ <u>**Colossians 1:13-18:**</u> "He has delivered us from the power of darkness and conveyed *us* into the kingdom of the Son of His love, in whom we have redemption through His blood, the forgiveness of sins. He is the image of the invisible God, the firstborn over all creation. For by Him all things were created that are in heaven and that are on earth, visible and invisible, whether thrones or dominions or principalities or powers. All things were created through Him and for Him. And He is before all things, and in Him all things consist. And He is the head of the body, the church, who is the beginning, the firstborn from the dead, that in all things He may have the preeminence.

- The blood gives us access to God because Jesus Christ paid the price and took our place.
- The blood gives us position and relationship.
- The blood delivers us from the power of darkness.
- Even though we're in Him and have a position of authority, we work with Him every day in our relationship.
- We have escaped the power of darkness because of Jesus and our relationship with Him.
- We still live in this world, and the devils controlling the world, are still here, but we are in Jesus.

THE PRECIOUS BLOOD OF JESUS

❖ **<u>Colossians 1:19-22:</u>** "For it pleased *the Father that* in Him all the fullness should dwell, and by Him to reconcile all things to Himself, by Him, whether things on earth or things in heaven, having made peace through the blood of His cross. And you, who once were alienated and enemies in your mind by wicked works, yet now He has reconciled in the body of His flesh through death, to present you holy, and blameless, and above reproach in His sight—

- This verse reveals that we were in captivity, and now we are not.
- The reality is people don't always know they're in captivity.
- They don't know that evil spirits have deceived them.
- You can see this among the unsaved or carnal Christians who are not walking with the Lord as they should.
- We want to be the ones to shed light on their lives.
- The world is under the power of satan and his evil spirit; he is the rebellious one.
- The basis of the kingdom of the power of darkness is a dictatorship.
- Paul is saying, you've been delivered from the power of darkness, and God has transferred you into the kingdom of the Son of His love.
- Because of the blood, our relationship with the Lord brings us favor, and it's based on love.
- Love is about a relationship with Him than it is about our position.
- Jesus is the exact representation of the Father, and whatever He did on the earth, we can do.

How has the blood of Jesus provided us access to a relationship with Him?

_____

_____

_____

_____

- That access has been given to us through the blood.

- Now that we have access, we must work in our relationship with Him.

- He is the image of the invisible God and the firstborn over all creation.

- God used Jesus to reverse the curse and bring us in.

- That's why we must preach the gospel and encourage people to walk with God in the power of the Spirit.

- satan doesn't want the Church to walk in the Spirit because He can't win against people that do.

- He can only come against those who walk in the flesh.

What do we receive out of our relationship with Him?

_____

_____

_____

_____

WE WERE MADE THROUGH HIM AND FOR HIM

DISCUSSION:

When Jesus took His blood to the mercy seat in heaven, He emptied it and kept His body. That's why He was able to walk for 40 days after He was resurrected. He was raised from the dead but hadn't ascended permanently to the Father. He was visiting. Paul is revealing that all things were created through Him. John 1:14 also talks about how Jesus tabernacled among us, and we beheld His glory. John was referring to when Jesus was on the earth after He was resurrected from the dead. He tells of those who embraced Jesus and how they listened to His teachings and obeyed Him. He describes how Jesus gave them the power and authority to become sons of God. John was saying all of this to reveal who we are in Him, what we have access to, and how we can have a manifestation of God in the flesh. The blood of Jesus is speaking very powerfully for us in heaven.

- If we look back to Collasians 1:16, "For by all things were created that are in heaven and that are on earth, visible and invisible, whether thrones or dominions or principalities or powers. All things were created through Him and for Him.

- Paul is explaining that Jesus is the beginning of all things.

- Everything that was made was made through Him from the beginning.

- He is the one that took our place, put Himself in a human body, and walked among us.

- It's not only believing that Jesus died on the cross; that's just the start of it.

- Your daily walk should reflect that you are discerning that He started all things.

- He is God; He is the one that thought of you before He even formed you.

- He wrote a book about you before He formed you.

- You were a desire and a thought in God, and then He breathed you out and created you.

- Everything that exists in this world was made through Him.

- He wrapped Himself in the flesh and came down.

- The blood of Jesus is spiritual blood that goes beyond time and space.

- It came before you were ever in existence.

How does knowing that Jesus thought of you before you were born and has a plan for you affect your daily walk?

_____

_____

_____

_____

ALL THINGS ARE CREATED BY JESUS

DISCUSSION:

In Colossians 1:16, Paul talks about thrones, dominions, principalities, and powers in the heavens. Paul was saying that Christ had everything to do with all that is in heaven and on the earth, whether visible or invisible, because He made them. There are powers under the earth, on the earth, and above the earth. There are dominions, levels, and echelons of demonic forces. We don't always understand these things. If we knew everything happening around us, it probably would be alarming. We don't see it all because it's being kept from us for a reason, but Jesus Christ made all these things. Everything that exists, whether it's good or bad, at one point was good. When He made things, He made them good, but things began to fall apart and deteriorate when the fall came.

- All things are created by Jesus Christ and through Him.
- It doesn't mean He created evil.
- What He created was good at the time He made it.
- We can't say that God created the terrible things we have today because He didn't do that.
- It became that way because our world is broken.
- He didn't create a hybrid race, but He created both entities involved.
- He is responsible for the original, which was good.
- When you read the story of creation, you can see that each time God created something, *it was good* (Genesis 1:1-31).
- He was before all things, and all things consist in Him

Explain in your own words how what is evil was once good.

_____

_____

_____

_____

JESUS, THE HEAD OF THE BODY

- Jesus is the head of the church and the firstborn from the dead.

- At the end of this age, the church on the earth is the culmination of His plan.

- That is because He wanted a family, a body.

- He redeemed the body of Christ, the glorious church.

- Jesus is the head of the body.

- He came and redeemed everything, then went back and sat at the right hand of the Father God.

- He expresses Himself and His plan through His body on the earth.

- The Holy Spirit came and is enforcing what was done.

- He is responsible for being the head of the body.

- We are here on the earth, and everything goes through us, the church.

- The church is the beginning, the firstborn from the dead, that in all things, He may have the pre-eminence.

- That's why we still emphasize Jesus as much as we do because He is the head. He's been given the name above all names.

- There is no higher name than His name.

- He was the fullness of God dwelling in a body was so that He could reconcile all things to Himself.
- His blood speaks at the throne.

What was Jesus' plan from the beginning in creating us?

_____

_____

_____

_____

- No matter what's going on, in the heavens or on the Earth or anywhere, reconciliation has come.
- If you don't see that happening in certain areas or with certain entities, then it's because they're in rebellion.
- The evil entities are in the heavens, visible and invisible.
- If all these rulers, visible or invisible, do not side with God, they're in rebellion.
- Colossians 1:19 says, "He's reconciled everything to Himself, whether things on the Earth or in heaven, having made peace through the blood of His cross."
- Jesus reconciled everything to Himself, so if you don't see things being reconciled to God, then we know that there must be invisible authorities as well as visible authorities operating.
- In leadership and through different agendas from entities and various groups, we see that they are in rebellion.
- They're not accepting the authority of God in their lives, in their countries, or in the world

- What you don't see, unless the Lord opens your eyes, is the spiritual hierarchy that's influencing it.

- The blood reconciled everything to God, and that is the absolute truth.

- Anything you see that's not responding to this is your enemy.

- Whether it's physical or spiritual, there's rebellion.

- When Jesus reconciled everything to Himself, He made peace through the blood.

- The Hebrew word for peace is *Shalom*. He made Shalom, so nothing is missing and nothing is broken.

- Everything is healed. Everything is delivered. Everything is paid for and debt-free. That's Shalom!

- Everything is in order, synchronized, in harmony, and you're not sick or tormented by demons. Everything is working in synchronization with heaven.

- You know it's the enemy when you don't see these things happening.

- It's written in the scriptures to Christians, so they can see that they've been transferred out of darkness.

- Christians don't adhere to the Kingdom of darkness anymore.

Why did Jesus reconcile everything to Himself? What does it look like when something is not responding to Jesus and His reconciliation?

_____

_____

_____

_____

THE PRECIOUS BLOOD OF JESUS

DISCUSSION:

Jesus didn't go with the way the system worked. He didn't fit in or work with the Pharisees. He worked against them because they were part of the world system. If you study people who start religions at the inception, they're powerful people, but they become cold and ineffective after a while because of the world system and the spirit of this world. According to scripture, the blood reconciles everything. The precious blood of Jesus is speaking, and it's causing a blessing to happen where there would be a curse. When you obey God, He will make way for you, and He will help you reach full reconciliation. Things have already been established, but sometimes the enemy doesn't listen when a decree has gone forth; you have to enforce it. People don't always do the right thing, and you need to help them by enforcing the decree. Jesus wasn't received by everyone. They killed Him for what He said, but it didn't change Him or who He was. He was resurrected, and He sits at the right hand of God, and that's how the separation came to be. We get punished and persecuted because we have sided with God. The evil spirits ruling this world will cause a stir with you. When you don't compromise, you'll stay right in there with the Lord where you're supposed to be.

- Before you believed in Jesus, you were held captive and separated from God through the world system.
- If you were to forget what Jesus did for you, the world system and the spirit of this world would be right there to take you in.
- It's important to know what evil spirits do to isolate people from receiving God's help.
- The devil works on people, so they forget their salvation and what they were delivered from.

- He wants them to forget the truth and that they've been reconciled.

- The spirit of this world promotes wicked works in the minds of the unredeemed, and people who are alienated and isolated can get trapped in their minds.

- Jesus reconciled you through the blood.

- When you placed your faith in Him, you were translated out of the world system.

What can we learn through Jesus and how He dealt with the world system?

_____

_____

_____

_____

- We need to remember what we were delivered from.

- We need to remember what it was like to be held captive.

- We must be aware that satan is a world dictator.

- He's a manipulator, and he does things by forcing you, pressuring you, and making you do things.

- You'll know when evil spirits are operating because you'll start to feel like you're being controlled.

- Their goal is to make God ineffective in this life.

- God has synchronized you with heaven now, and you can't go back to your old ways.

- The blood continues to work and speak, but you must renew your mind, be diligent and not compromise.

❖ I've seen this so many times in church history, where evil spirits have influenced people to start a movement. You can see their mindset being manipulated from behind the scenes, but they don't always know. It's hard to talk to deceived people and get them to see that the wrong spirit is influencing them. They need to be told the truth, but they might reject it.

- Peter warned us that once we escape the world's corruption through salvation in Christ, we are to avoid getting tangled back up and enslaved by sin again (2 Peter 2:20).
- You must be reminded of your reconciliation with God every day.
- Peter reveals the warfare going on and reminds them that they have been delivered.
- Most Christians don't understand the hierarchy of spiritual beings.
- They don't always understand how they operate or what's going on around them in the spirit.
- The early church leaders understood and made the people aware of this.

What happened to you when you chose Jesus and came out of the world system?

_____

_____

_____

_____

- Colossians 1:22 says, "In the body of his flesh through death to present you Holy and blameless and above reproach in His sight.

- Jesus' whole plan was to present us to the Father, Holy and blameless and above reproach.

- The only possible way is if we're separate from the world.

- The blood has separated us and made us holy.

- We are blameless when we're separate and not attached to the world.

- We identify with Jesus through His death, and it becomes like our death.

- We crucify our flesh, not allowing it to dominate.

- That alone causes separateness.

- The blood of Jesus causes holiness to come forth.

- It causes deliverance from the forces of evil.

- Deliverance comes when the blood is applied.

- When you remind yourself what you've been delivered from, you won't return to those things.

- The demons are waiting for you to come back, and if you do at your own will, they have permission to do something to you.

- When you resist demons, they have to flee from you.

- They can't do what they want to do unless you permit them.

How were you presented blameless and holy?

_____

_____

_____

_____

CHAPTER SEVEN

Grounded and Steadfast

*And you, who once were alienated and enemies in your mind by wicked
works, yet now He has reconciled in the body of His flesh through death, to
present you holy, and blameless, and above reproach in His sight— If
indeed you continue in the faith, grounded and steadfast, and are not moved
away from the hope of the gospel which you heard, which was preached to
every creature under heaven, of which I, Paul, became a minister.
— Colossians 1:21-23*

DISCUSSION:

Every day we must remind ourselves that we are separate from the world. We've
been delivered from the dictator of this world because of Jesus' sacrifice at the cross.
The blood of Jesus is what sets you apart as holy. The plan was that Jesus would be
seen here, coming through the body of believers, at the end of the age. He would be
the head of the Church, and we would be working in the end time as His ministry on
the earth. It's not about individual ministries and individuals; it's about the body of

Christ being built up in the unity of the faith. It's about getting people into their destiny and what God has called them to do. Christianity is not a one-time encounter with the cross; there must also be an application. It's about applying, experiencing, and encountering the Word of God in our lives. We're not just hearing about it and surviving down here; we need to know that we are effective. We are holy and set apart. Paul said that being grounded and steadfast in your faith will cause you to be holy, blameless, and above reproach. You received that through the death of Jesus Christ, but you're only going to be blameless and above reproach if you continue in the faith. You are anchored to the ground and immovable. Do not compromise or be moved away from the hope of the gospel which you have heard.

- ❖ **Colossians 1:24-28:** "I now rejoice in my sufferings for you, and fill up in my flesh what is lacking in the afflictions of Christ, for the sake of His body, which is the church, of which I became a minister according to the stewardship from God which was given to me for you, to fulfill the word of God, the mystery which has been hidden from ages and from generations, but now has been revealed to His saints. To them God willed to make known what are the riches of the glory of this mystery among the Gentiles: which is Christ in you, the hope of glory. Him we preach, warning every man and teaching every man in all wisdom, that we may present every man perfect in Christ Jesus."

  - God came to the Earth and fulfilled every desire and demand that the law and sin required.
  - Jesus met that demand, and it was paid.

- Whenever you experience difficult times in life, do not forget how good God is and what He's done for you!

- The blood is enough.

- You have full access to God through Jesus Christ.

- The mystery is the church at the end of the age, on the earth.

- The mystery revealed is Jesus Christ in you.

- You are supposed to proclaim this good news.

- When you announce it, you're not only declaring it to people; you're stating it to evil spirits.

- You're revealing that their judgment is pending, and they are coming to nothing.

- You're saying they've been destroyed and pronounced judged.

- You're to preach the good news to people and tell them that Christ is in them.

- Concentrate on Him and not on everything the devil is doing.

- Even if the devil is wreaking havoc around you, you must concentrate on what God says about you and that you are in Him.

- Focus on the treasure that's in you. If you do that and build others up, they can overcome.

- If you teach people to watch what the devil is doing all the time, then you'll be looking for the devil to do something.

- If you're looking for it, you will always see something bad.

- Paul's gospel was not about that at all. He said, remember where you came from, but concentrate on Christ in you, the hope of glory.

According to Colossians 1:23, what do we do with the gospel message?

_____

_____

_____

_____

OUR INHERITANCE

❖ **2 Corinthians 1:22:** "set his seal of ownership on us, and put his Spirit in our hearts as a deposit, guaranteeing what is to come."

- Paul said that there's a deposit given to us, guaranteeing that the full payment will come.
- The deposit is the Holy Spirit.
- We have a deposit, and we know that we will get the full payment one day, which means we're going to be in glory with Jesus Christ because we're co-heirs with Him.
- We have an inheritance, and we're going to stand with Him.
- As Jesus receives His inheritance, we get ours because we are fellow heirs of God and co-heirs with Jesus.
- We're going to stand in line and receive an inheritance that Jesus bought for us.
- We have the Holy Spirit's deposit in us now, guaranteeing that we're going to get the full payment.

What have we received, and how did we get it?

_____

_____

_____

_____

DISCUSSION:

In Ephesians 4, Paul talks about the fivefold ministry of the Church and how they are to build up the body into the unity of the faith. The three things that the fivefold ministry of the church should display are unity, maturity, and being built up. Paul strived to do that. In Colossians 1:28-29 Paul said, "Him we preach, warning every man and teaching every man in all wisdom, that we may present every man perfect in Christ Jesus. To this *end* I also labor, striving according to His working which works in me mightily." The end of his labor is that people would be presented perfect in Christ. He worked mightily doing this, and we are too as well. We want to be effective for change. We want to be effective for transformation; we do that by getting people to agree with God. If people don't know what you're saying, they can't agree with it. That's why Paul said that you need to have someone to interpret your tongues in a church service or meeting because otherwise, no one will know the meaning, and people won't be able to agree with what has been said (1 Corinthians 14:27-28). If you're going to speak in tongues, pray that you can interpret so that everyone can say *Amen* to what you've said.

What was Paul striving towards when he preached Christ? How can we ensure that we effectively assist with people's transformation?

_____

_____

_____

_____

WALKING OUT OUR FAITH

❖ Paul was given revelation on Mount Sinai in the Saudi Arabian desert. He wrote from that revelation reiterating that the blood of Jesus has caused us to be separate from the world.

- Jesus caused us to escape the corruption in the world.

- The blood has been applied, and it sets us apart.

- It also helps you in your mind because you are separate from that spirit that bound you. Therefore, your mentality is changing.

- Jesus reconciled us back to God, and He did this through His flesh.

- He presents us holy and blameless, but we must stay in faith.

- We have to do things according to the Spirit now.

- "Walking it out" is an important part.

- Paul says to encounter blamelessness and holiness above reproach; you have to continue in the faith by staying grounded and steadfast.

- You have to be a good soldier.

How are we set apart, and what are we set apart from?

_____

_____

_____

_____

GOD KNOWS ALL THINGS

❖ <u>**1 Peter 1:1-2:**</u> "Peter, an apostle of Jesus Christ, To the pilgrims of the Dispersion in Pontus, Galatia, Cappadocia, Asia, and Bithynia, elect according to the foreknowledge of God the Father, in sanctification of the Spirit, for obedience and sprinkling of the blood of Jesus Christ: Grace to you and peace be multiplied.

- Peter calls the people the elect. He says they're the elect according to the foreknowledge of God.

- Foreknowledge means that God already knows everyone that will choose Him.

- Predestination is knowing ahead of time.

- Predestination means that everyone is supposed to come to Heaven, and it's God's will, but He already knows the ones who are His because He is God.

- He doesn't let that interfere with offering salvation to all, even though

- He knows certain people won't choose Him.

- He knew Pharaoh wasn't going to cooperate with Moses, and He sent all those plagues.

- He sent Moses ten times, but Pharaoh didn't work with him.

- The Bible says that God hardened Pharaoh's heart.

- God kept telling Pharaoh, this is the way it is, and Pharaoh's heart got hardened.

How are the elect chosen?

_____

_____

_____

_____

- God, through Jesus Christ, made Salvation available so that everyone can come in because He's a just God.

- He doesn't pick and choose people to go to hell and heaven; that's Calvinism, and it's against scripture.

- God's foreknowledge doesn't stop Him from still offering salvation because He's a just God.

- There is a setting apart with the sanctification of the Spirit, and there's obedience.

- The children of Israel were obedient when they left Egypt, whereas Pharaoh was disobedient.

- God sees the blood of a spotless lamb on the altar, and He looks at Jesus blood and says, "You're blameless. You're set apart, and you're mine."

What is missing in a person's life who has a hardened heart?

_____

_____

_____

_____

INCORRUPTIBLE SEED

❖ <u>**1 Peter 1:3-4:**</u> "Blessed *be* the God and Father of our Lord Jesus Christ, who according to His abundant mercy has begotten us again to a living hope through the resurrection of Jesus Christ from the dead to an inheritance incorruptible and undefiled and that does not fade away, reserved in heaven for you, who are kept by the power of God through faith for salvation ready to be revealed in the last time.

- Jesus did it all because of His abundant mercy. That's a lot of mercy.
- Abundant mercy and the resurrection caused Jesus to triumph.
- We were raised with Him.
- The inheritance that we received from Him is incorruptible.
- It doesn't have a due date; you don't have to throw it away after a certain point.
- If you don't use it, it's held in heaven for you.
- It's incorruptible, and it's undefiled, and it doesn't fade away.
- We have that inheritance because of what Jesus did.
- The blood of Jesus speaks on our behalf, but it's not just speaking about salvation and whether we're going to hell or not.

- His blood has given us an inheritance that is not corrupt, it won't be defiled, and it's not going to fade away.

- Heaven is protecting your inheritance.

- Everything is yours, and it's all in heaven.

- While you're here, you're supposed to stay in the faith and remain steadfast.

- It's hard to get depressed or feel bad when you think about how your Father made everything, and He has given you His wealth and all that you need.

What are the benefits of our inheritance?

_____

_____

_____

_____

- ❖ **1 Peter 1:3-4:** "who are kept by the power of God through faith for salvation ready to be revealed in the last time."

  - Down here, you are kept by the power of God.
  - The power of God wants to preserve you and lead and guide you.
  - The power of God causes things that are shut to open.
  - It causes things that are dried up to be watered again.
  - Everywhere you go, the Spirit wants to open things up.
  - He's also revealing Himself, which will be revealed this last time.

- I look forward to Jesus revealing Himself to me. I look forward to what salvation means in these last days, and I look forward to seeing the doors open!

What does the power of God do for us as believers?

_____

_____

_____

_____

- The blood of Jesus isn't hard to understand. The inheritance was given to you by His blood.
- You can't silence the blood, and you can't silence the Spirit.
- The Spirit is always speaking, and He wants to reveal all the mysteries to you in these end times.
- Part of that mystery is Christ in us, the hope of glory.
- It has to do with incorruptible seed.
- The Word of God inside of us is incorruptible.

In what ways can you unveil the mysteries of Christ?

_____

_____

_____

_____

DISCERNING WHAT YOU HAVE

❖ <u>**1 John 1:1:**</u> "That which was from the beginning, which we have heard, which we have seen with our eyes, which we have looked upon, and our hands have handled, concerning the Word of life—"

- John is sharing with us that he met Jesus and beheld Him.
- Jesus was from the beginning. He is the eternal God, and He is the Word, incarnate.
- The apostles and disciples got to be with Jesus every day, but they didn't discern Him how they were writing about Him.
- When they were with Him, they were in discovery mode.
- Jesus was the Word from the beginning. He was the bread of life.
- He was the Word of life. He was spiritual, and He came to earth in the flesh.
- The apostles and disciples beheld Him physically. He was the Word of Life.
- That's why the devil fights you so much.
- He wants us to fight between the physical and spiritual realms to cause issues with our beliefs.
- God is Spirit, and those who worship must worship Him in spirit and truth (John 4:24).
- Jesus did everything in the flesh so that we can do it too.

CHAPTER EIGHT

Fellowship with God

That which was from the beginning, which we have heard, which we have seen with our eyes, which we have looked upon, and our hands have handled, concerning the Word of life— *the life was manifested, and we have seen, and bear witness, and declare to you that eternal life which was with the Father and was manifested to us— that which we have seen and heard we declare to you, that you also may have fellowship with us; and truly our fellowship is with the Father and with His Son Jesus Christ. And these things we write to you that your joy may be full. This is the message which we have heard from Him and declare to you, that God is light and in Him is no darkness at all. If we say that we have fellowship with Him, and walk in darkness, we lie and do not practice the truth. But if we walk in the light as He is in the light, we have fellowship with one another, and the blood of Jesus Christ His Son cleanses us from all sin. If we say that we have no sin, we deceive ourselves, and the truth is not in us. If we confess our sins, He is faithful and just to forgive us our sins and to cleanse us from all unrighteousness. If we say that we have not sinned, we make Him a liar, and His word is not in us.*

— 1 John 1:1-10

DISCUSSION:

Like Paul and Peter, John had a revelation after Jesus departed and went to be with the Father in heaven. John spent intimate time with Jesus and understood that Jesus was eternal. You can see the difference in the writings of the other disciples. It seems that John is more descriptive in his book and has more doctrine and theology than the others. John comes from the perspective that Jesus originated from heaven, He manifested to us, and we beheld the Father through Him. It's what Jesus was trying to convey. He said this repeatedly to the disciples, and finally, He says to Philip, "If you've seen me, you've seen the Father" (John 14:9). Jesus would share with the disciples that the Father is manifesting His works in us. Maybe they didn't understand it at the time, but they realized after the fact what was happening. We can say the same thing about ourselves, even though Jesus was saying it all along. In his book, John is speaking from revelation, but when he was with Jesus, he might not have understood everything. We can agree that we don't understand many things at the time, but because of what we encounter, we know more and more every day. John is saying, we beheld Him, we have fellowship with one another, and we have fellowship with the Father and with the Son. It's all been reconciled. Together we can get things done while we're here on Earth. That's why Jesus was talking about agreeing as touching any one thing. John writes that our joy would be full, he talks about separation and being delivered from darkness.

- Jesus' ministry was to restore fellowship between Him, the Father, and us.
- When the blood of Jesus is applied to a group of people like the body of Christ, and we believe it, we have access together.
- This means we can agree as touching anything and it's going to be done for us (Matthew 18:19).
- We can pray and agree.

- We can bind and loose.
- Our fellowship is with the Son and the Father through the Holy Spirit, but it's because the blood was applied.
- In this case, John is setting us up to understand what our purpose is.

How does our fellowship with God affect our relationships with the body of Christ?

_____

_____

_____

_____

HAVING FELLOWSHIP WITH THE LIGHT

- We have God in us.
- God is light. There's no darkness in Him.
- If we have fellowship with Him, we can't have fellowship with darkness.
- We can't walk in the light and simultaneously walk in the darkness.
- We don't practice the truth and then lie.
- John said if we have fellowship with Him, but we walk in darkness, we lie and do not practice the truth.
- The apostles were convinced that the blood of Jesus separated us, the light of God came in, and that we're not part of the world system.
- We are separate, so we can't practice evil.
- We can't walk in the world system.

- We can't be in darkness and say we are part of the light.
- If we walk in the light as He is in the light, we have fellowship with one another.
- The blood of Jesus Christ cleanses us from all sin.
- The body of believers is washed in the blood and set apart.
- If we walk in the light as a fellowship, then we have communion, and we encounter the Trinity, but we also encounter each other and have fellowship.
- We can fellowship and have unity becuase we have everything in common.
- Unity is what satan fights.
- If we're all believers in Jesus Christ, we're all under the blood.
- The blood sprinkled on us is all we need.
- We have fellowship with one another and the blood of Jesus Christ cleanses us from all sin.

How does the light bring unity in the body?

_____

_____

_____

_____

WALKING IN THE LIGHT

- John said, "If we say that we have no sin, we deceive ourselves and the truth is not in us." He's talking to believers here. He's talking to people that are having fellowship with one another and with God.

- As a believer, you can't say you don't have sin.

- If we say we don't have sin, we're deceived, and we're lying.

- The blood of Jesus cleanses us from all sin, but you have to acknowledge that you have sin in order for it to be cleansed.

- We don't willfully sin.

- We still deal with this broken world, and we can't say that we don't have sin because we have challenges every day.

- We have things that happen, whether it's commission or omission, whether you do something or you don't do something.

- If you omit something you were supposed to do, it's just as wrong.

- There are things that you don't know you do.

- There are unconscious things that you do that are wrong, and there are conscious things that you do that are wrong.

- John is saying we have to walk in the light.

- Part of what that means is we're confessing our sins.

Is it still considered a sin if it's overlooked?

_____

_____

_____

_____

What can you do about the sin in your life? He is a just God willing to forgive you.

_____

_____

_____

_____

- As believers, we can't say that we're perfect or don't need to confess our sins anymore.

- If you've done something wrong and you have fellowship with God, then you will know if you're wrong or not.

- The Holy Spirit will tell you that you need to confess your sin and that you've fallen short.

- Sin affects everyone else around you.

- 1 John 1:9 says, "If we confess our sins, He is faithful and just to forgive us our sins and to cleanse us from all unrighteousness."

- John is talking to believers. It's not talking about the condition of sin where you're going to hell. It refers to the experience of being on the earth and falling short.

- For us to say that we don't fall short of the glory of God is being deceived.

- To say that we don't need help anymore and that we're perfect is being deceived. We need help.

- If we say that we have not sinned, we make Him out to be a liar, and His Word is not in us. This is for people that have been forgiven and think they're perfect.

- John is saying we need to confess our sins.

THE PRECIOUS BLOOD OF JESUS

- We have fellowship with one another, so whatever we do affects others.

- When someone does something wrong, it affects other people.

- The body of Christ gets affected by it.

- We have fellowship with Him and with one another, and we walk with Him in the light as He is in the light.

- We have fellowship, and the blood of Jesus cleanses us from all sin.

❖ I've noticed that it seems insignificant with the way people think and believe. I've seen the damage that's done with this kind of false thinking and false doctrine where you think that you are sinless. You're always going to be dealing with this broken world, and there are traps. There is a lot of pressure, but you have to do the right thing. It's not always easy to do that. It's required by the Holy Spirit to have fellowship with the Father and with the Son.

   - You have to walk in the light.

   - In the light, darkness will be pushed out.

   - Everything gets revealed in the light.

   - If you sin, own it and confess it. Say, "I'm wrong," and then change whatever is wrong.

   - The blood of Jesus cleanses us from all sin, so we acknowledge the blood, and we are accountable.

   - To say that we don't sin, means that we're deceived and lying, and we make Him out to be a liar because God says you have fallen short.

   - You need the blood to be applied, and you need to acknowledge that every day.

DISCUSSION:

Deception is happening in the body of believers. You'll encounter people saying, "I confessed my sins; therefore, I'm righteous." Then they go and live the way they want to. They're constantly causing problems. That kind of doctrine puts them off by themselves where they have no one to be accountable to, and we all are accountable to each other. The body of believers is tied together. The reason why we're not seeing the power of God manifest in a strong way is that we're not having fellowship with the Father and the Son in its purest sense. When the Lord sheds light on it, we need to confess. We're not being accountable, and as a result, we suffer individually *and* corporately. The individuals are not reconciling with God, and they aren't reconciling with one another. People are being harmed in the body because we're not being accountable. We each need to have powerful fellowship in the Spirit with the Father and the Son. We've been reconciled by the blood of Jesus.

How does our fellowship with the Trinity hold us accountable?

_____

_____

_____

_____

LIVING A SET-APART LIFE

- To be separate from the world, we have to acknowledge that the blood separates us.

- We have to be aware that baptism separates us.

- We have to acknowledge that the Spirit separates us.

THE PRECIOUS BLOOD OF JESUS

- You have the blood, the water, and the Spirit, and they're all testifying that you are set apart.
- When the light of God is introduced, you can't walk in darkness.
- You can't do the things of the world and sin and say that you're with God.
- You have to say, "no".
- You have to say no to ungodliness and worldly passions.
- You have to say, "no, I'm set apart."
- It's YOU that must decide that.
- Then the Spirit will help you and work with you because you decided to do the opposite instead of being tempted.
- The Spirit starts to coach you and walk you through it.
- The blood speaks of your forgiveness and your separateness.
- Baptism does as well. When we go down under the water and come up, we come up with resurrection power.
- You have the Word speaking, the Spirit speaking, the blood speaking, and the light of God illuminating your way.
- The blood of Jesus works with the Word, it works with the water, and works with a mandate that God came into the world as light.
- He's working with you.
- The light of God is shining on you, and you have fellowship with the light.

How are we set apart by God, and what He has given us?

_____

_____

_____

_____

How do we live a set-apart life?

_____

_____

_____

_____

- You have fellowship with the Word.

- You have fellowship with the Spirit.

- You have fellowship with the blood.

- You have fellowship with the water of baptism.

- We're all baptized into the body of Christ.

- All of this is permanent in heaven. God has already done this, and it's already been established.

- Jesus is seated now, waiting for all of this to manifest in the body.

- That's why we need to build each other up, learn our lessons, and study the Word until we develop the maturity to teach it.

- It will come to a point where everyone will know it's time.

- Jesus will return when we have done the preaching of the gospel, and the harvest has come in.

- In the meantime, we do our part and preach the gospel.

What is Jesus waiting for us to grasp and understand in the body of Christ?

_____

_____

_____

_____

PURCHASED BY THE BLOOD

❖ <u>**Acts 20:17-21:**</u> "From Miletus he sent to Ephesus and called for the elders of the church. And when they had come to him, he said to them: "You know, from the first day that I came to Asia, in what manner I always lived among you, serving the Lord with all humility, with many tears and trials which happened to me by the plotting of the Jews; how I kept back nothing that was helpful, but proclaimed it to you, and taught you publicly and from house to house, testifying to Jews, and also to Greeks, repentance toward God and faith toward our Lord Jesus Christ.

❖ <u>**Acts 20:22-24:**</u> "And see, now I go bound in the spirit to Jerusalem, not knowing the things that will happen to me there, except that the Holy Spirit testifies in every city, saying that chains and tribulations await me. But none of these things move me; nor do I count my life dear to myself, so that I may finish my race with joy, and the ministry which I received from the Lord Jesus, to testify to the gospel of the grace of God."

❖ **Acts 20:25-29:** "And indeed, now I know that you all, among whom I have gone preaching the kingdom of God, will see my face no more. Therefore I testify to you this day that I *am* innocent of the blood of all *men*. For I have not shunned to declare to you the whole counsel of God. Therefore take heed to yourselves and to all the flock, among which the Holy Spirit has made you overseers, to shepherd the church of God which He purchased with His own blood. For I know this, that after my departure savage wolves will come in among you, not sparing the flock. Also from among yourselves men will rise up, speaking perverse things, to draw away the disciples after themselves. Therefore watch, and remember that for three years I did not cease to warn everyone night and day with tears.

- It's interesting that he testifies that he's innocent of all men's blood. We know he was involved with killing Christians, but he said, "I am innocent."
- He saw that he was forgiven by the blood of Jesus.
- He realized that he was completely innocent.
- At the end of his life after all that happened, he's telling this to everybody in the Book of Acts.
- Then he says, "There are those who are coming in as Wolves." He warns them to take heed to themselves, and to all the flock among whom the Holy Spirit has made overseers."
- He's talking to all the leaders and saying to shepherd the Church of God.
- He's telling them to watch over the people, and watch over the body, that was purchased by the blood of Jesus.

❖ <u>**Acts 20:30 to 35:**</u> "So now, brethren, I commend you to God and to the word of His grace, which is able to build you up and give you an inheritance among all those who are sanctified. I have coveted no one's silver or gold or apparel. Yes, you yourselves know that these hands have provided for my necessities, and for those who were with me. I have shown you in every way, by laboring like this, that you must support the weak. And remember the words of the Lord Jesus, that He said, 'It is more blessed to give than to receive.'"

- We, as the church, need to think about the fact that we have all been purchased by the blood.
- We are to shepherd and take care of each other.
- We're supposed to protect each other.
- Paul's last words, as he testified before he left, were that he didn't know what was going to happen to him. He eventually was beheaded in Rome.

According to these verses from Acts 20, what caused Paul not to be shaken or moved by the tribulations that await him?

_____

_____

_____

_____

DISCUSSION:

I've been to the place in Rome where Paul was imprisoned and eventually beheaded. He made this speech knowing that he was going to go there, and from all the indications, he never left. He died there and was beheaded. His testimony was that we were all purchased and that we, as overseers, should shepherd the flock and protect that which was purchased by His blood. That was a very powerful statement that Paul made. He was sharing his heart at that time, and it was for those people, but we are taking over where Paul left off by preaching the gospel. Paul was sharing the real meaning of why he did what he did and what was going to happen after he left. It's so important for us to adhere to the doctrine that was preached by the disciples and the revelation they left for us given through Jesus Christ. We have a responsibility. We've been handed the baton to guard the flock, and we should enforce what scripture says.

- The blood of Jesus purchased us, and we need to protect that.
- We need to protect each other and believe that we can be effective.
- We put the apostles on pedestals, but they've gone to heaven, and can't influence this realm in their flesh anymore. We have their writings, so the only way they can influence us is if we reread what they wrote and then do it.
- Let's heed to what is being said by the apostles.
- Let's be sober-minded.
- Be diligent about your calling.
- If you could meet the apostles right now in heaven, they would encourage you to go back and talk about these things with everyone.

CHAPTER NINE

Blessed Communion

When the hour had come, He sat down, and the twelve apostles with Him. Then He said to them, "With fervent desire I have desired to eat this Passover with you before I suffer; for I say to you, I will no longer eat of it until it is fulfilled in the kingdom of God." Then He took the cup, and gave thanks, and said, "Take this and divide it among yourselves; for I say to you, I will not drink of the fruit of the vine until the kingdom of God comes." And He took bread, gave thanks and broke it, and gave it to them, saying, "This is My body which is given for you; do this in remembrance of Me." Likewise He also took the cup after supper, saying, "This cup is the new covenant in My blood, which is shed for you. But behold, the hand of My betrayer is with Me on the table. And truly the Son of Man goes as it has been determined, but woe to that man by whom He is betrayed!" Then they began to question among themselves, which of them it was who would do this thing.

— Luke 22:14-23

DISCUSSION:

Passover was a feast that the Jewish people celebrated every year in remembrance of the first Passover in Egypt when one plague killed the firstborn of each household. God told Moses that the angel of death would pass over the home of anyone who placed the blood of a lamb on their doorpost, and the plague would not affect them (Exodus 12:7-14). Passover is celebrated as a feast every year. Here in Luke 22, Jesus was celebrating Passover with His disciples, and they were questioning among themselves who was going to betray Jesus, rather than focusing on what was being said. In other accounts, Jesus whispered to John because John asked, "Lord, which one is going to betray you?" Jesus said, "It is the one whom I shall give a piece of bread when I have dipped *it,*" and Jesus handed the bread to Judas. The moment that Judas took that bread, satan entered him (John 13:26). Then he got up, and Jesus said, "Whatever you're going to do, do it quickly." Judas partook of the Lord's supper unworthily, and, as a result, he permitted satan to enter him. That's why Paul tells us not to partake of the Lord's supper unworthily because that will bring judgment on us (1 Corinthians 11:29).

- In Luke 22, Jesus tells His Disciples that He would not eat the Passover meal with them again until they were in the kingdom together. He told them to take the bread and divide it among themselves.
- Jesus broke the bread and said, "This is my body which was given for you. Do this in remembrance of me."
- He hadn't even been crucified, but He was saying, "My body has been given for you."
- He hadn't been slain yet, but wanted them to remember His body and blood each time they took the elements.

- He wanted them to remember that His body was given for them.

- It's the same way with the blood. He took the cup and said, "This cup is the new covenant in My blood which is shed for you."

- He was having them drink it.

- Remember when He told the crowd, "If you don't drink my blood and eat my flesh, you have no part of me" (John 6:53).

- Jesus did this because He was showing the people and telling them that He was literally from heaven and that there is spiritual food that comes from Him and you must eat of Him; He's the bread that came down from heaven.

- When you get together and have Communion, remind yourself of what Jesus said and did while you are having fellowship with each other.

- It will strengthen the relationship you have with the Lord and with one another.

Explain the intimacy with taking communion?

_____

_____

_____

_____

❖ <u>**1 Corinthians 10:14-17:**</u> "Therefore, my beloved, flee from idolatry. I speak as to wise men; judge for yourselves what I say. The cup of blessing which we bless, is it not the communion of the blood of Christ? The bread which we break, is it not the communion of the body of Christ? For we, *though* many, are one bread *and* one body; for we all partake of that one bread.

- What Paul is saying here is more serious than what people realize.

- He's asking them questions to get them to think and look at where they are.

- Paul is explaining to them that this is not just a meal.

- We are essentially partaking of one body and becoming one body together.

- It's a spiritual exercise. It's worship.

- The bread and the blood represent Christ's body and blood.

- Something happens to you when you take that in because there's a transfer inside us from the physical to the spiritual.

- People create a big gap between the physical and the spiritual, but Jesus did this for 40 days after He was resurrected.

- He preached in a body that had no blood in it, and He ate, and He walked through walls during these 40 days. He still went to heaven and presented His blood to the Father.

SEPARATING FROM THE WORLD SYSTEM

❖ <u>**1 Corinthians 10:18-22:**</u> "Observe Israel after the flesh: Are not those who eat of the sacrifices partakers of the altar? What am I saying then? That an idol is anything, or what is offered to idols is anything? Rather, that the things which the Gentiles sacrifice they sacrifice to demons and not to God, and I do not want you to have fellowship with demons. You cannot drink the cup of the Lord and the cup of demons; you cannot partake of the Lord's table and of the table of demons. Or do we provoke the Lord to jealousy? Are we stronger than He?

- Paul says, "You cannot drink the cup of the Lord and the cup of demons; you cannot partake of the Lord's table and the table of demons."

- He said this because people had not separated themselves from the world system.

- We have to acknowledge that the blood, baptism, the light of God, and the Spirit of God separate us from the world.

- When the baptism or the sprinkling of blood, or the Spirit of God, the anointing of God, the water, the Word, or the light, enter in, it separates us

- This needs to be taught.

- The table of the Lord was a time when there was a separation of knowledge.

- They were all together.

- It's something that was done in the early Church to experience being separate and having fellowship.

- It is a spiritual thing, not just a physical thing.

- To come to the table and bring the world with you in any way is just unthinkable, but that's what Judas did. He came to the table and ate unworthily.

- He brought something to the table that affected everyone.

- He didn't discern the body of Christ.

- He didn't discern the body of believers there.

- He made decisions and brought that to the table, and He was judged.

- As soon as he partook of it unworthily, satan entered him.

- He became the instrument to deliver Jesus over to be crucified.

- You can't come to the table of demons and then come to the table of the Lord.

- You can't drink of the cup of demons and then come to the table of the Lord and drink the cup of the Lord.

- Paul says, "Do we provoke the Lord to Jealousy? Are we stronger than He?"

- He is saying this because satan entered the whole group that was at the communion table.

What causes you to be separate, and how do you live it?

_____

_____

_____

_____

❖ <u>**1 Corinthians 11:23-33:**</u> "For I received from the Lord that which I also delivered to you: that the Lord Jesus on the *same* night in which He was betrayed took bread; and when He had given thanks, He broke *it* and said, "Take, eat; this is My body which is broken for you; do this in remembrance of Me." In the same manner *He* also *took* the cup after supper, saying, "This cup is the new covenant in My blood. This do, as often as you drink *it,* in remembrance of Me." For as often as you eat this bread and drink this cup, you proclaim the Lord's death till He comes. Therefore whoever eats this bread or drinks *this* cup of the Lord in an unworthy manner will be guilty of the body and blood of the Lord. But let a man examine himself, and so let him eat of the bread and drink of the cup. For he who eats and drinks in an unworthy manner eats and drinks judgment to himself, not discerning the Lord's body.

- Paul warned the table of the Lord is a sacred thing, and it affects you.

- If you don't judge yourself, you're going to be judged.

- Paul is instructing them because he cares for them.

- We're supposed to examine ourselves when we sit at the table of the Lord.

- If we haven't examined ourselves and eat and drink unworthily, we drink judgment to ourselves, not discerning the Lord's body, just like Judas did.

- He's explaining to us what Judas did when he ate and drank unworthily, he became guilty for delivering Jesus over, and His body was crucified.

- He became guilty of the blood and the body of Jesus Christ.

- Paul is saying to the people that if you come to the table and you think it's just food to eat or you're just doing it because you do it, if you come to the table in an unworthy manner, you could be guilty of that same thing.

- It's a strong statement, but you can't water it down. That's what it says here.

How does sin affect the whole body when you come to the table unworthily?

_____

_____

_____

_____

What is it about communion that causes you to be affected when you take it unworthily?

_____

_____

_____

_____

❖ **1 Corinthians 11:30-34:** "For this reason many *are* weak and sick among you, and many sleep. For if we would judge ourselves, we would not be judged. But when we are judged, we are chastened by the Lord, that we may not be condemned with the world. Therefore, my brethren, when you come together to eat, wait for one another. But if anyone is hungry, let him eat at home, lest you come together for judgment. And the rest I will set in order when I come.

- Paul continues by saying, "For this reason, many are weak and sick among you, and many sleep."

- How in the world could this be happening in the Church?

- Many are weak and sick among you, and many sleep.

- The word sleep used in these references is talking about dying early.

- He is saying that they are weak and sick and dying early because they are eating and drinking judgment to themselves, not discerning the Lord's body.

- Now that you know this, it will help you take Communion more often.

- When you do just examine yourself and discern the Lord's body and eat, it worthily.

- Communion is healing to your body because of the blood and the body of Jesus.

- People must judge themselves and stop judging others.

- When you start telling people what to do and instruct them in this way, you will be able to discern whether they are in the wrong spirit by their response; they will go into a rebellious kind of attitude.

What is the cause for people in Verse 30 getting sick and dying?

_____

_____

_____

_____

- **Verse 31-32** says, "If we judge ourselves, we will not be judged, but when we are judged, we are chastened by the Lord that we may not be condemned with the world."

- Paul reminds us that we should not come to the table of the Lord hungry; we should take care of that at home first because that's not the purpose of Communion.

- It's not about eating.

- He said that if you do that, it's part of the wrong attitude, and you're going to come together in judgment.

- In other words, you're all going to be in trouble because of one person.

- He said, "The rest I will set in order when I come."

- He went to visit them.

- We need to help each other. We need to be responsible for each other in this.

- We need to have more times of Communion and fellowship.

- If people are taught correctly, they won't do it unworthily.

- According to what Paul is saying, this is very serious, but it's also very beneficial if you do it right.

What should we be doing before we come to the table of the Lord?

_____

_____

_____

_____

DISCUSSION:

I don't want to discourage you from partaking in Communion. You should do it as often as you wish, but you should also know it is serious. We're coming into a covenant when we do it, and it's a spiritual exercise. Something very powerful will happen over this. People often ask, "Can I take Communion by myself? Do I have to do it in Church? Do I have to do it with a priest or with a Minister?" You can take it alone. You can take it with your spouse. You could take it with other ministers or in Church. You can take it anywhere, and there is no limit on how often you can take it! However, you don't want to take it with the wrong attitude or do it so often that you are just going through the motions. That could cause trouble for you if it's not heartfelt or if you do it in an atmosphere where there is irreverence.

For instance, I probably wouldn't take it at a restaurant unless I could be certain I wouldn't be interrupted. It's the same way with doing it all the time. You don't want to get in the habit of saying, "Oh, I have to take Communion now." This is how religious spirits get in. Something is good, to begin with, but then it becomes a demand or something done out of obligation. That's my main warning and concern when addressing people's questions about the ritual when observing these types of spiritual practices.

- If it's a holy and sacred thing to you, you can do it as many times as you wish.
- The question is, why are you doing it?
- It should be something sacred every time.
- I pray a lot. I pray at different times of the day, and I observe it as being sacred each time.
- I don't just do it out of obligation. I do it because I want to.
- If you can do that with Communion, then do it.
- All I'm saying is to be mindful of others who are with you and explain it to them so that they know what they're doing.

THE BLOOD BRINGS US NEAR TO HIM

❖ **Ephesians, 2:11-13:** "Therefore remember that you, once Gentiles in the flesh—who are called Uncircumcision by what is called the Circumcision made in the flesh by hands—that at that time you were without Christ, being aliens from the commonwealth of Israel and strangers from the covenants of promise, having no hope and without God in the world. But now in Christ Jesus you who once were far off have been brought near by the blood of Christ.

- One of the things that they practiced in Israel was circumcision.

- This procedure separated them from all the other people in the world, and God instituted it in Israel.

- The Israelites observed circumcision, but the Gentiles—the non-Jewish people groups— did not adhere to it.

- It was an outward sign that God did to set them apart.

- Paul addresses that now we have a circumcision of the heart.

- The Spirit does it, and it sets us apart.

- It's a spiritual thing, not just a physical thing.

- The Gentiles didn't practice circumcision once they became Christians and came into covenant.

- In **Verse 12**, Paul addresses this when he says, "At that time, you were without Christ, being aliens from the commonwealth of Israel and strangers from the covenants of promise, having no hope and without God in the world. But now, in Christ Jesus you who once were far off, have been brought near by the blood of Christ."

- It's not like we had to travel anywhere. It happened inside of us.

- The Spirit circumcised our hearts, and then the blood of Jesus gave us access.

- This is important for today because people must realize it's not something that we do outwardly as far as our salvation or setting ourselves apart.

- Of course, believers will behave differently in their actions, their character, and how they conduct themselves.

What is the purpose of circumcision? How is circumcision observed in Christianity?

_____

_____

_____

_____

DISCUSSION:

When people would ask me why I do not participate in certain activities, I would say, " I don't want to do that; I'm a Christian. I've been set free from that and I'm set apart." That would be kind of foreign and weird to them. They would respond with, "Don't you want to have fun and do this?" They were captured by the spirit of the world. They were deceived into thinking that because I didn't do those things, I was different and didn't have fun or enjoy life, but to me, they were different because they did those things. I know that they were wrong, but they didn't see themselves as wrong. They believed that now participating was wrong.

- It's important for God's people to be circumcised in their hearts.

- It's not an outward thing; however, it will manifest itself in a person's lifestyle.

- Then, you can tell them, "This is why I am the way I am."

- You can preach the gospel and tell them why you are the way you are.

- People that judge you for being separate from the world are essentially saying God's wrong.

- They have deception and rebellion in them.

- Paul explained that non-Christians are strangers who are outside the covenant and the promise.

- Before we entered into salvation, we had no hope and were without God.

- Now we have been ushered into God's presence through the blood.

- Now, it's a local call instead of a long-distance call.

- God is right inside of us, and the gap has been closed.

- We've been brought near through the blood.

How can we be a hope for others living in the world?

_____
_____
_____
_____
_____
_____

Now that you are part of the covenant and promise, what do you have according to Ephesians 2:11-13?

_____
_____
_____
_____
_____
_____

CHAPTER TEN

The Manifestation of Faith

And without faith it is impossible to please God, because anyone who comes to
him must believe that he exists and that he rewards those who
earnestly seek him.
— Hebrews 11:6 NIV

DISCUSSION:

A separateness causes us to be different, and it manifests in our lives. Paul talked about it in Hebrews 11; it is referred to as "the faith chapter." The observation of the people's faith is being proclaimed. It's talking about true faith. It's what they did. That's why the blood is so effective in your life if you choose to discern it as that. It is a process now of you walking with God. Hebrews 11 is all about the manifestations of faith in these people's lives.

❖ **Hebrews 11:27:** "By faith he forsook Egypt, not fearing the wrath of the king; for he endured as seeing Him who is invisible."

- Paul is talking about Passover and the sprinkling of blood.

- He's also talking about Moses. It says, "He forsook Egypt, and he didn't consider the wrath of Pharaoh. He endured Him who was invisible."

- Moses forsook Egypt in that he was leaving his people and his career. He was leaving Egypt, not the Israelites.

- He wasn't an Egyptian. He was adopted.

- He was no longer considering himself as being part of Pharaoh's court.

- He endured because he saw Him who was invisible.

- We hear about the blood of Jesus and about our faith in Jesus, but the real separateness occurred when the plague came, and it didn't touch the Israelites.

- They escaped Egypt, and they escaped the plague because they set themselves apart as the people of God.

- In the Bible, Egypt is a symbol of the world.

- To avoid the effects of the plague, the Israelites had to sacrifice an animal and put the blood of that animal on the doorpost.

- That's the kind of faith we're talking about; obedience to what God says.

- They were instructed to obey Him, and they had faith that they would be saved if they listened.

- We see this same faith throughout Hebrews 11; God's people overcame by their faith.

- God gave them instructions, and then they had to choose to obey.

- This type of obedience is what made them separate from the world.

- They went with God and obeyed Him.

- This obedience was attributed to faith and resulted in God performing many miracles.

How was faith manifested in the lives of the Israelites concerning Passover?

_____

_____

_____

_____

FAITH SHIFTS ATMOSPHERES

- All these people were known for their faith in God because they all believed in Him who was invisible. Their faith manifested.

- That is how we see the blood manifest.

- If you meditate on these different chapters in this study guide, it won't be long before you see demons manifest.

- As soon as you get convinced about the reality of the blood of Jesus, something happens inside of you, and it shifts the atmosphere.

- There comes the point where that pressure from within and God's power will press the enemy and press the spiritual realm for manifestation.

- Something will have to move, and the Holy Spirit is not going to back off.

What caused the people's faith to manifest?

_____

_____

_____

_____

- If the Holy Spirit is expanding, and something is in the way, the point will come where your faith and your participation will cause things to manifest.

- Because you meditated on the word of God and the blood of Jesus, and you applied the blood, and you used the name of Jesus, it's only a matter of time before things start to manifest for you.

- At times it may appear that you just swatted a Bee's nest.

- Meditating on the Word of God, praying in the Spirit, doing the right thing, and making a heartfelt agreement with the Word of God causes a manifestation outwardly.

- Things begin to happen for you and around you.

- It's because everything that is spiritual must eventually come forth in the physical.

- It's done through faith.

- It's done because you are set apart, and the set-apartness comes through the blood of Jesus.

- Then the Spirit of God comes in and causes you to walk in separation.

- When we realize who we really are, and what has been done for us, and we get together with other believers, it's only a matter of time before towns and cities start to change.

- We need to teach and reinforce this message to people, and we will see the manifestation by conquering territories in the Spirit.

- It's very important to understand what we have coming.

- We need to acknowledge the blood of Jesus, apply it, and meditate on His name so that we can be separate from the world.

- We need to continue to grow and be enhanced by God's Word.

How do things begin to manifest outwardly in your favor?

_____

_____

_____

_____

FAITHFUL TO THE END

❖ **<u>Hebrews 12:22-24:</u>** "But you have come to Mount Zion and to the city of the living God, the heavenly Jerusalem, to an innumerable company of angels, to the general assembly and church of the firstborn *who are* registered in heaven, to God the Judge of all, to the spirits of just men made perfect, to Jesus the Mediator of the new covenant, and to the blood of sprinkling that speaks better things than *that of* Abel.

DISCUSSION:

Here in Hebrews 12, we see a snapshot of Mount Zion, the spiritual mountain where the city of the living God is. It's also where the heavenly Jerusalem will come down. I was taken to the throne room to see this culmination at the end of the age. All the saints were together. The angels were there, singing this song to the Lamb, Jesus. He was seated at the right hand of God. Hebrews is talking about this general assembly and Church of the Firstborn. That's what we're called, and we're registered to God, in heaven, in the Lamb's Book of Life. The blood has separated us and made us this amazing assembly, the church of the living God, the firstborn. We are registered and written in the Lamb's Book of Life. The God of the universe, the judge of all, is seated on His throne while all this happens. There are spirits of just men made perfect everywhere. These are all the people that lived before; they are being honored because of what they went through. They were purified, and they are honored now. We will be among them, and we will be purified, and we'll be honored. That's why I'm encouraging you to be diligent and faithful to the end, build yourself up in your most Holy of faith, and pray in the Spirit. All of this is happening right now. There's a throne where God sits. There are saints and angels and spirits of just men made perfect. There's an innumerable company of angels in the heavenly Jerusalem. It exists right now in heaven.

How does your faith play a part in connection with eternity?

_____

_____

_____

_____

THE PRECIOUS BLOOD OF JESUS

THE MEDIATOR

- Jesus, the Mediator of the new covenant, is at the right hand of God.

- He's called the mediator because He's the one that brings the parties together at the table for the covenant to be signed.

- He is the one that sits with the Father and introduces the body of believers, the ones that He purchased for the Father.

- He introduces us to Him, and we reconcile and agree together.

- He's the one that's in charge.

- He's the High Priest. He's the King. He was the sacrifice.

- It was His blood as the high priest that offered it up.

- He is now seated at a table as a mediator.

- When Jesus sent the Holy Spirit back, He called Him "the standby."

- Jesus called Him "the advocate."

- He called Him "the counselor." He is the Mediator. The Holy Spirit is the one who counsels us and helps us, and brings us together.

- It's a new covenant because a new agreement must be agreed upon and signed, and Jesus is the mediator.

- Jesus wants us to know the terms of the new covenant. His blood is speaking, and He is speaking, and He wants to usher us in.

What does Jesus do for us as The Mediator?

_____

_____

_____

_____

BLOOD HAS A VOICE

- Right now, the blood of Jesus is sprinkled, and it's speaking better things than that of Abel.

- Why was that said?

- When Abel was killed by Cain, God asked him where his brother was. Abel was dead, but the blood of Abel was speaking from the ground where it was spilled.

- God said, "The voice of your brother's blood cries out to Me from the ground" (Genesis 4:10).

- Blood has a voice.

- Jesus' blood is being sprinkled on everything in the new covenant, and that blood has a voice and is speaking right now.

- Jesus' blood is speaking better things than Abel's blood.

- It's louder, it's more effective, and it's the new covenant.

- Jesus is seated and bringing us all together.

- To be effective, we can never sit and say, "I'm set, I have enough knowledge, or I have enough understanding."

- Never be satisfied with where you are because there's so much more!

THE PRECIOUS BLOOD OF JESUS

❖ <u>**Hebrews 13:10-16:**</u> "We have an altar from which those who serve the tabernacle have no right to eat. For the bodies of those animals, whose blood is brought into the sanctuary by the high priest for sin, are burned outside the camp. Therefore Jesus also, that He might sanctify the people with His own blood, suffered outside the gate. Therefore let us go forth to Him, outside the camp, bearing His reproach. For here we have no continuing city, but we seek the one to come. Therefore by Him let us continually offer the sacrifice of praise to God, that is, the fruit of *our* lips, giving thanks to His name. But do not forget to do good and to share, for with such sacrifices God is well pleased.

- The Apostle Paul most likely wrote the book of Hebrews, but his authorship is not definite because there's no name on it, but it does bear the marks of Paul talking to the Hebrews.
- The author of Hebrews says, "Therefore let us go forth with Him outside the camp bearing His reproach." Why would he say that?
- It's about being separate.
- When we identify with Christ, we identify in His resurrection, and we also identify with His death.
- We should include ourselves with Him.
- If the world rejects us, it's because they rejected Him.
- We shouldn't try to get along with people that are rebellious. It's not for us to make that decision.
- We are to stand for Christ.
- We are to go outside and be separate.
- We are to come out from the world. It says we don't have a continuing city.

- That means there's not a city that's going to continue to operate. Everything is going to be destroyed. Everything is coming to nothing.
- We are seeking the one to come. We are seeking the heavenly Jerusalem.
- The heavenly Jerusalem will come down, and we're going to be part of that kingdom, so we go outside the camp.
- We leave the world, and we're separate from them.
- We say, "I'm waiting for the city whose builder and maker is God to come down."
- We are to worship and sacrifice with our lips, and we're to live by the fruits of our lips.
- Our fruit comes from our mouths.
- It comes from our words, and we offer it as praise unto God.

In Hebrews 13:10-16, what does it mean "to go outside the camp" with Christ?

_____

_____

_____

_____

- ❖ **Hebrews 13:22-23:** "Now may the God of peace who brought up our Lord Jesus from the dead, that great Shepherd of the sheep, through the blood of the everlasting covenant, make you complete in every good work to do His will, working in you what is well pleasing in His sight, through Jesus Christ, to whom *be* glory forever and ever. Amen.

- At the end of this letter, the writer is praying and blessing the people, and this is how we should pray over people and bless them.

- He called the Lord Jesus "the great Shepherd.

- He refers to the blood of His everlasting covenant.

- I want to emphasize that whatever it is that God has done, we only know in part. There's so much more that He's done that we still don't know.

- All that He has done is everlasting.

- Before Paul became Paul, he was Saul, and he was killing Christians, but in Galatians, he tells them, "I was set apart as an apostle since birth."

- When Paul wrote these letters, he didn't operate in the knowledge he had several years before that. He didn't know any of that, but it was always true.

How does it encourage you knowing Paul's history was nothing like his future?

_____

_____

_____

_____

- We don't know if Paul ever physically met Jesus when he was alive.

- He met Him in a vision when He appeared to him, and Jesus visited him and taught him, but we don't know that Paul ever saw Jesus when he was growing up as a boy.

- Paul didn't say he had seen Jesus at any one time.

- The everlasting covenant and the blood that was shed, are permanent forever, even when Paul was not operating correctly.

- Just like when you were in the world and you didn't know Jesus, but all that we know is true of His Word.

- When God does something, it's an everlasting covenant, so He agrees with us, and He's doing things for us, but we're not participating in it.

- The book of Revelation testifies about Jesus, who was the Lamb slain from the foundations of the world.

- Jesus was slain before we were even on the earth and before the earth was formed.

- That means that we're not operating at all in what we should be because God already knew what we needed, and He did it even if we weren't going to accept it.

- You're going to encounter an acceleration in the Spirit because of what's happening right now.

- The revelation is so much more available to you because the Word of God is being taught correctly, and there's an open heaven that we're encountering on the earth at this time.

- The revelation and what's available to you will come forth in a greater measure than you ever expected.

- Even when Paul wasn't operating in it, it was still true.

- Even when you weren't operating in this, it was still true.

- Now that you know and the revelation has come, think about how pleasing you're going to be to God.

- Through the blood of the everlasting covenant, you are made complete in every good work!

What does the everlasting covenant provide for you? How is your life marked by it even before you walk in the truth of it?

_____

_____

_____

_____

- It's going to make you complete to where you have good works; every good work to do His will.

- He's talking about manifestation here. It's going to become an action.

- It's working in you, but then it causes you to be well pleased in His sight.

- There's a manifestation of doing His will, which is doing every good work.

- It's not a good thought, it's a good work. It's a good manifestation.

- I look at people, and I can see God in their life. I can see Him moving. I can see Him doing things. That's how I can tell. It's the manifestation. It's the fruit.

SALVATION PRAYER

Lord God,
I confess that I am a sinner.
I confess that I need Your Son, Jesus.
Please forgive me in His name.
Lord Jesus, I believe You died for me and that You
are alive and listening to me now.
I now turn from my sins and welcome
You into my heart. Come and take control of my life.
Make me the kind of person You want me to be.
Now, fill me with Your Holy Spirit, who will show me how to live for You.
I acknowledge You before men as my Savior and my Lord.
In Jesus' name. Amen.

If you prayed this prayer, please contact us at
info@kevinzadai.com for more information and material.

We welcome you to join our network at Warriornotes.tv
for access to exclusive programming

To enroll in our ministry school, go to:
Warriornotesschool.com

Visit KevinZadai.com for additional ministry materials

About Dr. Kevin Zadai

Kevin Zadai, Th.D., was called to the ministry at the age of ten. He attended Central Bible College in Springfield, Missouri, where he received a Bachelor of Arts in theology. Later, he received training in missions at Rhema Bible College and a Th. D. at Primus University. He is currently ordained through Rev. Dr. Jesse and Rev. Dr. Cathy Duplantis. At the age of thirty-one, during a routine day surgery, he found himself "on the other side of the veil" with Jesus. For forty-five minutes, the Master revealed spiritual truths before returning him to his body and assigning him to a supernatural ministry. Kevin holds a commercial pilot license and is retired from Southwest Airlines after twenty-nine years as a flight attendant. Kevin is the founder and president of Warrior Notes School of Ministry. He and his lovely wife, Kathi, reside in New Orleans, Louisiana.

Other Books and Study Guides
By Dr. Kevin Zadai

Kevin has written over fufty books and study guides
Please see our website for a complete list of materials!
Kevinzadai.com

60-Day Healing Devotional

60-Day Devotional: Encountering the Heavenly Sapphire1

60-Day Devotional: Supernatural Finances

The Agenda of Angels

The Agenda of Angels Study Guide

A Meeting Place with God, The Heavenly Encounters Series Volume

Days of Heaven on Earth

Days of Heaven on Earth: A Study Guide to the Days Ahead

Days of Heaven on Earth Prayer and Confession Guide

Encountering God's Normal

Encountering God's Normal: Study Guide

Encountering God's Will

Encountering the Heavenly Sapphire Study Guide

From Breakthrough to Overthrow: Study Guide

Have you Been to the Altar Lately?

Heavenly Visitation

Heavenly Visitation: Study Guide

Heavenly Visitation Prayer and Confession Guide

How to Minister to the Sick: Study Guide

It's Rigged in Your Favor

It's all Rigged in Your Favor: Study Guide

It's Time to Take Back Our Country

Lord Help Me to Understand Myself:
Study Guide

Mystery of the Power Words

Mystery of the Power Words:
Study Guide

The Notes of a Warrior: The Secrets
of Spiritual Warfare Volume 1
Study Guide

The Notes of a Warrior: The Secrets
of Spiritual Warfare Volume 2
Study Guide

The Power of Creative Worship:
Study Guide

Prayer Nations
With Kevin & Kathi Zadai

Praying from the Heavenly Realms

Praying from the Heavenly Realms:
Study Guide

Receiving from Heaven

Receiving from Heaven:
Study Guide

Stories from the Glory
with Sister Ruth Carneal

Supernatural Finances

Supernatural Finances
Study Guide

Supernatural Prayer Strategies of a
Warrior: Study Guide

Taking a Stand
Against the Enemy

Taking Off the Limitations

Taking Off the Limitations:
Study Guide

The Vision and Battle Strategies of
Warrior Notes Intl.

Warrior Fellowships Season 1
Volume 1 Study Guide

Warrior Fellowships Season 1
Volume 2 Study Guide

Warrior Notes Aviation Volume 1:
Flight Manual Study Guide

Warrior Women
Volume 1 Study Guide

Warrior Women
Volume 2 Study Guide

Warrior Justice: A Study Guide to
Experiencing Freedom from
Demonic Oppression

You Can Hear God's Voice

You Can Hear God's Voice
Study Guide

Made in United States
Orlando, FL
01 April 2022

16370046R00080